THE BOOK OF PRESERVES

It's a delicious, back-to-nature experience to make your own preserves, and you know what's going into your jars. Fruit and vegetables in season give the best flavours and colours, and are better buys (unless, of course, you can pick your own crop)! You need only small quantities, as these are easier to work with and more controllable to cook. First, though, it's really important to turn the page and read our hints for success.

Pamela Clark
FOOD EDITOR

NOTE: *Conversion charts for cup and spoon measurements and oven temperatures are on page 125.*

EDITOR: Maryanne Blacker

FOOD EDITOR: Pamela Clark

DESIGN DIRECTOR: Neil Carlyle

■ ■ ■

DESIGNER: Louise McGeachie

■ ■ ■

ASSISTANT FOOD EDITORS: Jan Castorina, Karen Green

ASSOCIATE FOOD EDITOR: Enid Morrison

CHIEF HOME ECONOMIST: Kathy Wharton

HOME ECONOMISTS: Jon Allen, Jane Ash, Tikki Durrant, Sue Hipwell, Karen Hughes, Karen Maughan, Voula Mantzouridis, Alexandra McCowan, Louise Patniotis

FOOD STYLISTS: Rosemary De Santis, Carolyn Fienberg, Michelle Gorry, Jacqui Hing, Victoria Lewis, Anna Phillips

PHOTOGRAPHERS: Kevin Brown, Robert Clark, Andre Martin, Robert Taylor, Jon Waddy

EDITORIAL ASSISTANT: Elizabeth Gray

KITCHEN ASSISTANT: Amy Wong

■ ■ ■

HOME LIBRARY STAFF:

ASSISTANT EDITOR: Judy Newman

ART DIRECTOR: Robbylee Phelan

SECRETARY: Wendy Moore

■ ■ ■

EDITOR-IN-CHIEF: Sandra Funnell

PUBLISHER: Richard Walsh

■ ■ ■

Produced by The Australian Women's Weekly Home Library Division
Typeset by Letter Perfect, Sydney.
Printed by Dai Nippon Co Ltd, Tokyo, Japan
Published by Australian Consolidated Press, 54 Park Street Sydney
Distributed by Network Distribution Company, 54 Park Street Sydney
Distributed in the U.K. by Australian Consolidated Press (UK) Ltd (0604) 760 456. Distributed in New Zealand by Gordon and Gotch (NZ) Ltd (09) 654 397. Distributed in Canada by Whitecap Books Ltd (604) 980 9852. Distributed in South Africa by Intermag (011) 493 3200.

■ ■ ■

■ ■ ■

COVER: Clockwise from front: Mandarin Jelly Marmalade, page 43, Peach Jam, page 20, Raspberry Red Spread, page 119, Dark Plum Jam, page 16, Strawberry Jam, page 10, Apple Jelly, page 59. Fabric from Laura Ashley.
OPPOSITE: Plum Butter, page 118.
BACK COVER: Apple and Red Pepper Chutney, page 64.

HINTS FOR SUCCESS

Here are the tried and tested tips that will give you success every time; they are simple procedures that work perfectly, and it's important to read them before you start to cook.

JAMS AND CONSERVES

Jam is based on either one fruit or several different fruits. The fruit is cooked until tender, then sugar is added and the mixture is cooked until it will jell or become thick enough to spread when it is served at room temperature.

A conserve is a preserve made from whole or large pieces of fruit. It is made in the same way as jam.

Fruit for jams and conserves

Fruit should be as freshly picked as possible, and slightly under-ripe; at this stage the pectin (the setting agent in preserves) content is at its highest. For best results in jam making, make small amounts at a time. The shorter cooking time will give better results in flavour, texture and appearance. As a guide, avoid using more than 2kg fruit for any jam recipe.

The most suitable fruits for jam making are those which have a good balance of acid and pectin; however, lemon juice contains both pectin and acid, and can be added to fruits low in acid or pectin to improve the setting properties of the jam.

* *Fruits with good balance of acid and pectin are*: grapes, crab apples, currants, quinces, sour gooseberries, grapefruit, lemons, limes, sour apples, sour guavas, sour oranges, sour plums.

* *Fruits high in pectin and low in acid are:* sweet apples, sweet guavas, sweet quinces. When making jam or jelly from these particular fruits, add 2 tablespoons lemon juice to each 1kg fruit to increase the acid content.

* *Fruits low in pectin and high in acid are:* apricots, pineapples, rhubarb, sour peaches. When making jam from these fruits, add 2 tablespoons lemon juice to each 1kg fruit to increase the pectin content.

* *Fruits low in acid and pectin and not suitable without the addition of other fruits or juice for making jam are*: pears, melons, sweet peaches, most berries and cherries.

Equipment used for preserves

Use large wide-topped aluminium, stainless steel or enamel saucepans or boilers; do not use copper or unsealed cast iron pans because the acid in the preserve will damage the metal, and colour and flavour the ingredients. Do not leave vinegar or fruit or vegetable mixtures standing in aluminium pans for more than about an hour.

Jam making

There is a basic method for making jam if you can't find a suitable recipe. This will always work provided the fruit is at its peak for jam making and the pectin/acid content is balanced.

1. Wash fruit well, cut away any bruised or damaged parts. Chop or slice fruit, reserve seeds; these provide extra pectin for setting.

They can be soaked separately in a cup half full of water, then the seeds strained out and discarded. The gelatinous liquid left is added to the fruit. Seeds can also be tied in a muslin bag and cooked with the fruit; the bag is discarded later.

Citrus rind needs overnight soaking to soften; in this case fruit is cooked in the soaking liquid – see details for Marmalades, page 4.

2. Place fruit in pan; fruit layer should not be more than about 3cm deep (this allows rapid evaporation of liquid later). Add enough water to barely cover the fruit, cover pan, bring to boil over high heat, reduce heat, simmer gently to extract the pectin, acid and full flavour from the fruit. It is important that fruit be simmered until it is as tender as required; once the sugar is added, further cooking will not tenderise the fruit any more. This can take from about 10 minutes for soft fruit such as berries, or up to 1½ hours for tough citrus rinds.

3. Once the fruit or rind is tender, measure fruit mixture in a measuring cup, allow 1 cup sugar to each cup of fruit mixture.

4. Return fruit mixture to pan; it should not be more than about 3cm deep; bring to boil. Add sugar to pan; the mixture at this stage should not be more than about 5cm deep.

5. Stir fruit mixture over high heat to dissolve sugar quickly. Sugar **must** be dissolved before mixture boils or jam may crystallise. Use pastry brush dipped in water to brush down sides of pan and wooden spoon to remove every single grain of sugar.

6. Once sugar is dissolved, boil the jam as rapidly as possible for minimum time given in recipe or until the mixture is thick or will jell (see below). The time to jell can be some time between 10 minutes or up to an hour. Do not stir jam after sugar has dissolved, but use a wooden spoon to check that the jam is not sticking on the base of the pan, particularly towards the end of cooking time when jam is thicker. When jam has cooked for the required time, start testing to see if jam has jelled.

To test if jam has jelled

Dip a wooden spoon into the mixture, hold spoon up above mixture and tilt the bowl of the spoon towards you; as mixture cooks and thickens, the drops will fall more heavily from the spoon. When it is ready, two or three drops will roll down the edge of the spoon and join together in a heavy mass.

When this happens, remove jam or jelly from heat to stop further cooking. Drop a teaspoon of mixture onto a saucer which has been chilled in freezer for a few minutes, return saucer to freezer until jam or jelly is at room or serving temperature but not frozen.

* Jam which has pieces of fruit in it should have formed a skin which wrinkles when pushed with the finger.

*Jam which is pulpy in texture should be of a spreadable consistency.

*Jelly should be a firm mass on the saucer. If mixture does not jell, return to the heat, boil rapidly until mixture will jell when tested; this may take only a few more minutes.

7. When jam is at jelling stage, skim surface, if necessary. If jam contains pieces of fruit, let it stand for 5 to 10 minutes (depending on the size and type of fruit used) before bottling. This allows the mixture to cool slightly and the fruit to disperse itself more evenly.

* Marmalade usually requires the full 10 minutes standing time.

* Jams made from pulpy fruit should be bottled immediately.

Note: Jams and jellies will reach jelling point at 105 degrees C to 106 degrees C (220 degrees F to 222 degrees F). Any candy thermometer can be used.

8. Pour jam into hot sterilised jars right to the top of the jar, jam will shrink on cooling.

9. Seal jars when cold. Label jam and store in a cool dark place. If jam has been cooked and sealed correctly, it will keep for at least 12 months. Once opened, store in refrigerator.

If jam has not set

This is due to an imbalance of pectin and acid; or insufficient evaporation in the cooking process. Lemon juice can be added and jam re-boiled until it will jell when tested.

However, if jam has darkened in colour and has a caramel taste (which happens when sugar is overcooked) it cannot be re-boiled.

If the flavour is still palatable, commercial pectin (available in powdered form from health food stores, some supermarkets, and hardware stores which sell home preserving equipment) will set the jam; follow the directions on the packet. Different brands are available; see Glossary, page 125.

JELLIES

A good jelly should be clear and translucent, firm enough to hold its own shape, but soft enough to quiver when cut with a spoon. The strained juice from the cooked fruit is combined with sugar, then cooked to a point at which it will set when cold.

For information about fruit and equipment for jelly making, see under Jams and Conserves.

Basic steps in jelly making

1. Wash fruit thoroughly, cut away any bruised or damaged parts. Chop fruit roughly, stems, seeds, skin and all.

2. Place prepared fruit in pan; fruit layer should not be more than 3cm deep. Add enough water to barely cover fruit, so fruit just begins to float.

3. Cover pan, bring to boil over high heat, reduce heat, simmer gently, covered, until fruit is tender and just beginning to become pulpy. The time varies, depending on type and ripeness of fruit, between 30 minutes and 1 hour.

4. Strain fruit mixture through a fine cloth. There are several easy methods of doing this:

* A cone-shaped jelly bag with attachments for hanging can be bought from specialist kitchen stores; have it thoroughly damp before use.

* A jelly bag can be made by turning a chair or stool upside down on a table; tie corners of a square of damp fine cloth (boiled unbleached calico, an old tea towel, muslin, or piece of sheeting) securely to the legs of the chair, leave cloth loose enough to dip in the centre.

Place a large bowl under the bag or cloth. Pour the fruit and its liquid into the bag or cloth; do not push or force the fruit through, as this will cause the jelly to be cloudy. Cover the fruit loosely with greaseproof paper or tea towel to protect from dust and insects, leave liquid to drip through cloth; this will take up to 12 hours.

* If you are in a hurry, and not too concerned about the clarity of the jelly, the easiest,quickest way to strain fruit is through a large strainer or colander suspended over a bowl. Pour fruit mixture into strainer, press fruit with a wooden spoon to extract as much liquid as possible; discard the fruit pulp. To remove any remaining pulp from liquid, place a clean piece of damp fine cloth inside a strainer over a deep bowl, pour the liquid into cloth and allow it to drip through; do not force the liquid through the cloth.

5. Measure the liquid in a measuring

cup; determine how much sugar is required, according to recipes (generally ¾ cup or 1 cup sugar to each cup of liquid, depending on the pectin content of the fruit). If not following a recipe, this pectin test will indicate the amount of sugar required.

TO TEST FOR PECTIN CONTENT

Place 1 teaspoon of the strained fruit liquid in a glass, add 3 teaspoons methylated spirits; stir mixture gently with a teaspoon. We coloured about 1 tablespoon of the fruit liquid so it would show up clearly in the photograph. The liquid is normally almost colourless.

* If mixture forms a fairly solid single jelly-like clot, the fruit liquid is high in pectin; in this case use 1 cup sugar to each 1 cup of liquid. (This jelly will set quickly, without long cooking time; there will be little evaporation of liquid, giving a good yield of jelly for the amount of fruit used.)

* If several smaller clots of jelly form, the jelly is not high in pectin; use ¾ cup sugar to each 1 cup fruit liquid.

* If pectin test fails to produce any clots, or gives a mass of tiny clots, it will then be necessary to add some fruit juice naturally rich in pectin, usually 2 tablespoons fresh strained lemon juice to each 1kg fruit; add this after the sugar is dissolved.

6. Return fruit liquid to pan, there should not be more than 3cm covering base of pan.

7. Bring fruit liquid to the boil over high heat, add sugar, stir without boiling until sugar is dissolved; do not allow mixture to boil until sugar is dissolved or mixture may crystallise. All sugar grains must be brushed from sides of pan and from wooden spoon; use a pastry brush dipped in water to do this. Heat must be kept high to dissolve sugar quickly for best results.

8. When mixture comes to the boil, leave on high heat. Boil as rapidly as possible, uncovered, without stirring, for minimum time suggested in individual recipes. (These times are only a guide, as every batch of jelly will reach jelling point at a different time depending on ripeness of fruit; constant watching and testing is necessary.) See Jams and Conserves.

9. Jelly should foam up high in the pan, and high heat must be maintained without allowing the mixture to boil over. (This explains the need for a large pan.)

10. When mixture jells, allow bubbles to subside, lift off any scum which has appeared on the surface (it is wasteful to remove scum during cooking time). Use a jug to pour jelly in a slow, steady stream down the side of hot sterilised jars. Work quickly or jelly will set in pan. Do not stir or move the jelly too much with the jug, or jelly will not be clear.

11. Fill jars right to the top; jelly will shrink slightly on cooling.

12. Seal jars when cold. It will take at least 12 hours for jelly to become cold. Label and date jars, store in a cool dark place. Jelly should keep for 12 months. Once a jar is opened, keep refrigerated.

If jelly has not set

This is due to a lack of pectin and/or acid. Re-boiling will cause the jelly to lose its clarity and texture; the addition of commercial pectin will also spoil its appearance, but will at least make the jelly set; follow directions on packet. If all else fails, jellies can be set by using a commercial dessert-type jelly. These jellies need to be stored in the refrigerator and will not keep long term.

Choose a similar flavour and colour to the home-made jelly, place the jelly crystals in a saucepan with ½ cup water, stir over low heat until dissolved: do not boil. Add the unset home-made jelly and stir over low heat until any lumps are melted. The amount of jelly crystals required will, of course, depend on the consistency and quantity of the home-made jelly. As a guide, one 85g packet of jelly crystals should set about 3 cups home-made jelly.

MARMALADES

Marmalade is a clear jelly preserve with small pieces of rind or thin slices of fruit suspended in it. Marmalades are made from citrus fruits, or a combination of fruits, one or two being citrus. The name is said to have come from the Portuguese word for quince, marmelo.

Many marmalade recipes suggest fruit be sliced thinly, water added, and fruit soaked overnight. This extracts pectin and begins the process of softening the rind. If time does not permit overnight soaking, simply cook for longer than recipe instructs, but be careful not to evaporate an excessive amount of liquid or the balance of ingredients will be upset. Do not soak fruit in aluminium, cast iron or copper pans.

Some recipes require the seeds to be soaked and then boiled with the fruit; seeds are rich in pectin. (See rules for Jams and Conserves.)

Fruit, with the water in which it was soaked, is cooked, covered, over a low heat until the rind is tender; this will take somewhere between 30 minutes and 1½ hours, depending on thickness and toughness of rind. Once sugar is added, further cooking will not tenderise the rind, so be sure rind is as tender as desired before the sugar is added.

Follow detailed instructions for jam making when making marmalades; fruit can also be minced, blanched or chopped in a food processor.

JARS, STERILISING, SEALING AND STORAGE

Jars: Jars must be glass, without chips or cracks; and should be sterilised. As a general rule, hot preserves go into hot sterilised jars, cold preserves go into cold sterilised jars. Jars must always be dry. Tea-towels and your hands must be clean when handling jars. Unclean jars can cause deterioration in all preserves.

To sterilise jars: In dishwasher, use rinse cycle and hottest temperature, do not use detergent.

Without a dishwasher:

Method 1: Place clean jars lying down in pan, cover completely with cold water, cover pan, bring to boil and boil, covered, for 20 minutes; carefully remove jars from water (thick rubber gloves and tongs are useful for this); drain well, stand right way up on wooden board. The heat from the jars will quickly evaporate any water remaining in the jars.

Method 2: Wash jars well in hot soapy water, rinse thoroughly in hot water to remove soap. Stand jars right way up on board in cold oven (do not allow jars to touch); turn oven to very slow, leave for 30 minutes, remove jars from oven.

To seal jars: When preserve is cold, it must be correctly sealed to prevent deterioration. Ordinary metal lids are not suitable; the acid content of the preserve will corrode the lids and the contents will be inedible. Special lined and treated or lacquered lids, available with home preserving outfits, are suitable for sealing. Plastic screw-top lids give a good seal (plastic snap-on lids are not airtight enough). Plastic lids must be well washed, rinsed and dried. Some older preserving outfits have glass lids; these can be sterilised by either of the above methods. Do not use aluminium foil, cellophane or paper covers for preserves; foil will be corroded by the acid in the preserves and paper and cellophane are not airtight enough for long term keeping.

Paraffin wax (available from chemists) makes an excellent seal. Melt over low heat, pour a thin layer about 2mm just enough to cover surface, leave until almost set, then pour another thin layer on top of the first layer. Insert small pieces of string into wax just before it sets to make it easier to remove wax later. It is important not to over-heat wax, or it will shrink on cooling, giving an imperfect seal. Wipe sealed jars clean, label and date.

Storage: Store preserves in a cool, airy, dark, dry place (light can cause deterioration) until required. Once a jar has been opened, all preserves must be stored, covered, in the refrigerator. If you live in a wet humid climate, the best storage place is the refrigerator.

CHUTNEYS, PICKLES, RELISHES AND SAUCES

These are all condiments made from vegetables, fruits, sugar, spices and vinegar. With these preserves, it is often necessary to secure whole spices in a muslin bag to be cooked with the preserve. This bag is discarded later.

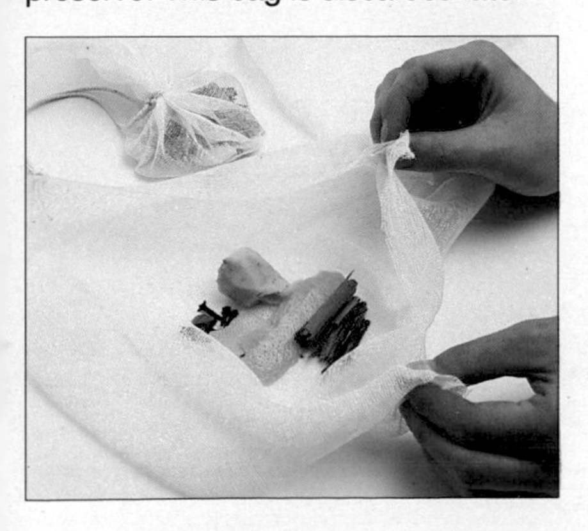

VINEGAR

Use good-quality malt vinegar; cheap vinegars do not contain enough acetic acid to act as a preservative. Good vinegar contains at least 4 per cent acetic acid. Follow the same rules for Jams and Conserves for which type of pan to use, condition of fresh produce and bottling, sealing and storing.

SUGAR

Sugar is the ingredient that preserves these home-cooked products. The only difference is in the colour and how that colour affects the finished preserve.

White sugar is used for jams, jellies, conserves and marmalades. Crystal sugar (white table sugar), castor sugar (finer) and loaf sugar can all be used with the same results. Castor sugar will dissolve faster than the other 2 varieties. We have specified when to use castor sugar; other than that, use crystal sugar.

Brown and white sugars are used in chutneys, pickles, relishes, sauces, etc. Brown or black sugar simply gives a richer colour and flavour.

If you want to enter your jam or jelly into a competition and have it at its sparkling best, warming the sugar will help you achieve clarity. The theory is the faster the sugar is dissolved and the faster the jam or jelly reaches jelling point, the better looking the preserve will be.

To warm sugar: Spread sugar into a baking dish, it should not be more than about 3cm deep. Place dish into slow oven for about 10 minutes, stir the sugar occasionally to distribute the warmth evenly.

LEMON JUICE

This is rich in pectin and acid, and can make or rescue a sweet preserve. See information on Jams and Conserves. Lime juice is just as rich in pectin and acid and can be substituted for lemon juice at any time.

GRAPES

When we have referred to black grapes, they are purplish to red in colour, white grapes are pale green in colour.

BERRIES AND CURRANTS

Freshly picked, slightly under-ripe perfect fruit is always the best; however, frozen fruit can be substituted. If you don't have scales it is handy to know that 250g berries will fill a 250ml measuring cup.

APPLES

We have used Granny Smith apples throughout this book. Try to obtain apples which are as freshly picked as possible and preferably under-ripe. Apples which have been in cold storage will not give you good results.

SUGAR-FREE PRESERVES

Throughout this book we have included some preserve recipes which do not contain sugar. Some contain artificial sweeteners. These recipes must be kept, covered, in the refrigerator and will keep for only about 4 weeks.

MICROWAVE COOKERY

We have not given instructions for microwave cookery in this book. However, jams, conserves, marmalades and jellies can all be cooked in a microwave oven. As a guide, do not use more than 500g fruit at the one time, follow the same method as in conventional recipes. Also remember there is minimal amount of evaporation with microwave cooking and most preserves depend on this at the last stages of cooking. Always use a large shallow container, cook, covered or uncovered as the recipes state, check the preserve constantly during the cooking time. The flavour and colour of microwave cooked jams, etc, is excellent. The golden rule is keep checking the preserve as it cooks.

Chutneys, pickles and sauces can also be cooked in small quantities in the microwave oven but, as evaporation is a necessary part of the process, we prefer to cook these preserves in the conventional way.

Relishes are usually fine to microwave; the colour retention is excellent.

Butters and spreads can be cooked in a microwave oven but require careful monitoring during microwave cooking as the butters must not boil and the spreads are thick and tend to overcook quickly. We prefer to cook butters and spreads conventionally.

JAMS & CONSERVES

Start saving jars now, ready for the year-round pleasures of making jams and conserves. Choose fruit in season when it is most plentiful and cheapest (or use a good crop from your own garden). Fresh stone fruit and berries give the best results, but frozen fruits are a fairly good substitute. Before you start, it's important to read our hints for success on pages 2 to 5.

MELON AND LEMON JAM

2 large (4kg) jam melons, peeled
3 medium (540g) lemons
2 litres (8 cups) water
8 cups (2kg) sugar

Cut melons in half, discard seeds, chop flesh into small cubes, place in large bowl (you will need 2kg flesh).

Finely grate rind from lemons (you will need 1½ tablespoons rind). Cut lemons in half, remove and reserve seeds. Peel away white pith, chop flesh. Place pith with reserved seeds in a piece of muslin, tie securely. Add rind, lemon flesh and water to melon cubes in bowl, add muslin bag, cover; stand overnight.

Transfer mixture to large saucepan, bring to boil, simmer, covered, for about 45 minutes or until melon is pulpy; discard muslin bag.

Add sugar to pan, stir over heat, without boiling, until sugar is dissolved. Bring to boil, boil, uncovered, without stirring,for about 45 minutes or until jam jells when tested. Pour into hot sterilised jars; seal when cold.

Makes about 8 cups.

RASPBERRY AND PEACH JAM

500g raspberries
2 medium (300g) peaches, peeled, chopped
1½ cups sugar
2 teaspoons grated lemon rind
¼ cup water
2 tablespoons port

Combine berries, peaches, sugar, rind and water in large saucepan. Stir over heat, without boiling, until sugar is dissolved. Bring to boil, boil, uncovered, without stirring, for about 15 minutes or until jam jells when tested. Stir in port, pour into hot sterilised jars; seal when cold.

Makes about 3 cups.

DRIED APRICOT AND PUMPKIN JAM

250g dried apricots, chopped
1 litre (4 cups) water
375g pumpkin, peeled, chopped
¼ cup lemon juice
2 tablespoons chopped glace ginger
4 cups (1kg) sugar

Combine apricots and water in bowl, cover, stand overnight.

Combine undrained apricots, pumpkin, juice and ginger in large saucepan. Bring to boil, simmer, covered, for about 20 minutes or until pumpkin is soft. Stir in sugar, stir over heat, without boiling, until sugar is dissolved. Bring to boil, boil, uncovered, without stirring,for about 30 minutes or until jam jells when tested. Pour into hot sterilised jars; seal when cold.

Makes about 6 cups.

RIGHT: Clockwise from front: Raspberry and Peach Jam, Melon and Lemon Jam, Dried Apricot and Pumpkin Jam.

PER ALIMENTI
ITALCAPS

SUGAR-FREE PEAR AND BLUEBERRY JAM

Jam will keep refrigerated for 2 weeks.

500g blueberries
2 medium (300g) pears, peeled, chopped
2 tablespoons lemon juice
2 teaspoons white vinegar
2 teaspoons liquid sweetener
2 tablespoons Jamsetta
½ teaspoon tartaric acid

Combine berries, pears, juice and vinegar in large saucepan.

Bring to boil, simmer, covered, for about 25 minutes or until fruit is soft. Stir in remaining ingredients. Bring to boil, boil, uncovered, for about 5 minutes or until jam jells when tested. Pour into hot sterilised jars; seal when cold.

Makes about 1½ cups.

SUGAR-FREE BERRY JAM

Jam will keep refrigerated for 2 weeks. We used blackberries in this recipe, but any type of berries would be suitable.

1kg berries
¼ cup lemon juice
2 teaspoons liquid sweetener
1 pouch (20g) Gelfix

Combine berries and juice in large saucepan. Bring to boil, simmer, covered, for about 15 minutes or until fruit is soft. Stir in remaining ingredients. Bring to boil, boil, uncovered, for about 10 minutes or until jam jells when tested. Pour jam into hot sterilised jars; seal when cold.

Makes about 3 cups.

RIGHT: From back: Sugar-Free Pear and Blueberry Jam, Sugar-Free Berry Jam.

STRAWBERRY JAM

1½kg strawberries, hulled
½ cup lemon juice
5 cups (1¼kg) sugar

Combine all ingredients in large saucepan, stir over heat, without boiling, until sugar is dissolved. Bring to boil, simmer, uncovered, without stirring, for about 20 minutes or until jam jells when tested. Pour jam into hot sterilised jars; seal when cold.

Makes about 5 cups.

BOYSENBERRY LIQUEUR JAM

Any berry can be used in this recipe.
1kg boysenberries
4 cups (1kg) sugar
1 cup lemon juice
3 tablespoons Cointreau

Combine berries, sugar and juice in a large saucepan, stir over heat, without boiling, until sugar is dissolved. Bring to boil, boil, uncovered, without stirring, for about 25 minutes or until jam jells when tested. Stir in liqueur, pour into hot sterilised jars; seal when cold.

Makes about 5 cups.

CHERRY REDCURRANT JAM

500g cherries
600g redcurrants
⅓ cup water
2¾ cups sugar, approximately

Halve cherries, remove stones. Remove stems from currants. Combine cherries, currants and water in large saucepan. Bring to boil, simmer, covered, for about 25 minutes or until fruit is soft.

Measure fruit mixture, allow ¾ cup sugar to each cup of fruit mixture.

Return fruit mixture and sugar to pan, stir over heat, without boiling, until sugar is dissolved. Bring to boil, boil, uncovered, without stirring, for about 15 minutes or until jam jells when tested. Pour into hot sterilised jars; seal when cold.

Makes about 3 cups.

NUTTY TROPICAL FRUIT JAM

2 medium (500g) mangoes, chopped
1 small (500g) papaw, chopped
⅓ cup lemon juice
3 cups sugar, approximately
½ cup pine nuts
1½ tablespoons Kirsch

Combine mangoes, papaw and juice in large saucepan, bring to boil, simmer, covered, for about 10 minutes or until fruit is soft.

Measure fruit mixture, allow 1 cup sugar to each cup of fruit mixture.

Return fruit mixture and sugar to pan, stir over heat, without boiling, until sugar is dissolved. Bring to boil, boil, uncovered, without stirring, for about 15 minutes or until jam jells when tested. Stir in nuts and liqueur, stand for about 10 minutes, stirring occasionally, or until nuts remain suspended in jam. Pour into hot sterilised jars; seal when cold.

Makes about 3 cups.

BELOW: Strawberry Jam.
RIGHT: Clockwise from front: Cherry Redcurrant Jam, Nutty Tropical Fruit Jam, Boysenberry Liqueur Jam.

PER ALIMENTI

DRIED FRUIT JAM

1½ cups (150g) chopped dried apples
1 cup (150g) chopped dried peaches
3 cups (500g) chopped dried figs
1 litre (4 cups) water
1 teaspoon grated lemon rind
2 cinnamon sticks
1½ litres (6 cups) water, extra
½ cup lemon juice
11 cups (2¾ kg) sugar

Combine fruit, water, rind and cinnamon in large bowl, cover, stand overnight.

Combine undrained fruit mixture, extra water and juice in large saucepan. Bring to boil, simmer, covered, for about 15 minutes or until fruit is soft. Measure fruit mixture, allow 1 cup sugar to each cup of fruit mixture.

Return fruit mixture and sugar to pan, stir over heat, without boiling, until sugar is dissolved. Bring to boil, boil, uncovered, without stirring, for about 50 minutes or until jam jells when tested. Discard cinnamon sticks. Pour jam into hot sterilised jars; seal when cold.

Makes about 11 cups.

MELON AND PASSIONFRUIT JAM

You need about 6 passionfruit.

1 small (1½ kg) jam melon, peeled, chopped
6 cups (1½ kg) sugar
⅓ cup lemon juice
½ cup passionfruit pulp

Combine melon with half the sugar in large bowl; stand overnight. Combine melon mixture, remaining sugar and juice in large saucepan. Stir over heat, without boiling, until sugar is dissolved. Bring to boil, boil, uncovered, without stirring, for 30 minutes. Stir in passionfruit, boil further 5 minutes or until jam jells when tested. Pour jam into hot sterilised jars; seal when cold.

Makes about 6 cups.

ABOVE: From back: Melon and Passionfruit Jam, Dried Fruit Jam.

China from Shop 3, Balmain; linen and silver spoon from Cameo Antiques.

TROPICAL TREAT JAM

You need about 3 passionfruit.

5 large (1kg) apples
3 medium (500g) pears
3 medium (500g) bananas, chopped
1 small (500g) pineapple, chopped
½ cup lemon juice
1⅓ cups orange juice
6 cups (1½kg) sugar
¼ cup passionfruit pulp

Peel, core and chop apples and pears. Tie apple and pear skins and the cores in a piece of muslin.

Combine apples, pears, bananas, pineapple, juices and muslin bag in large saucepan, bring to boil, simmer, covered, for about 20 minutes or until fruit is soft. Discard bag.

Add sugar, stir over heat, without boiling, until sugar is dissolved. Bring to boil, boil, uncovered, without stirring, for about 1 hour or until jam jells when tested. Stir in passionfruit, stand 5 minutes before pouring into hot sterilised jars; seal when cold.

Makes about 8 cups.

DRIED APRICOT ORANGE JAM

500g dried apricots, chopped
1½ litres (6 cups) water
2 tablespoons grated orange rind
⅔ cup orange juice
2 tablespoons lemon juice
8 cups (2kg) sugar

Combine apricots and water in bowl, cover, stand overnight.

Combine undrained apricots, rind and juices in large saucepan. Bring to boil, simmer, covered, for about 20 minutes or until apricots are soft. Stir in sugar, stir over heat, without boiling, until sugar is dissolved. Bring to boil, simmer, uncovered, without stirring, for about 1¼ hours or until jam jells when tested. Pour into hot sterilised jars; seal when cold.

Makes about 8 cups.

LEFT: From left: Tropical Treat Jam, Dried Apricot Orange Jam.

FRUIT SALAD JAM

You need about 6 passionfruit.

1 medium (390g) grapefruit
1 large (220g) orange
4 medium (340g) limes
2 cups water
1 small (500g) pineapple
4 medium (500g) apples, peeled, chopped
1 litre (4 cups) water, extra
3½ cups sugar, approximately
½ cup passionfruit pulp

Remove rind from grapefruit, orange and limes, cut rind into very thin strips. Combine rind and water in bowl. Remove and discard pith from grapefruit, orange and limes. Using sharp knife, cut flesh into segments, reserving any juice. Reserve seeds, tie in a piece of muslin, add to bowl with rind, cover; stand overnight.

Combine undrained rind mixture, segments and juice, pineapple, apples and extra water in large saucepan. Bring to boil, simmer, covered, for 1 hour.

Measure fruit mixture, allow ¾ cup sugar to each cup fruit mixture.

Return fruit mixture and sugar to pan, stir over heat, without boiling, until sugar is dissolved. Bring to boil, boil, uncovered, without stirring, for about 20 minutes or until jam jells when tested. Discard bag of seeds. Stir in passionfruit. Stand 10 minutes, stirring occasionally. Pour into hot sterilised jars; seal when cold.

Makes about 6 cups.

DARK PLUM JAM

28 medium (2kg) blood plums
1 litre (4 cups) water
⅓ cup lemon juice
6 cups (1½ kg) sugar

Cut plums into quarters, remove stones. Combine plums and water in large saucepan, bring to boil, simmer, covered, for 1 hour.

Add juice and sugar to pan, stir over heat, without boiling, until sugar is dissolved. Bring to boil, boil, uncovered, without stirring, for about 20 minutes or until jam jells when tested. Pour into hot sterilised jars; seal when cold.

Makes about 8 cups.

APRICOT AND MINT CONSERVE

38 medium (1½kg) apricots
3 medium (540g) lemons
½ cup water
6 cups (1½kg) sugar
1 tablespoon white vinegar
2 tablespoons chopped fresh mint
2 teaspoons grated fresh ginger

Halve apricots, remove stones. Break open a quarter of the stones, remove kernels, lightly crush kernels, reserve. Squeeze lemons, reserve the juice and the seeds.

Tie reserved kernels and seeds in muslin bag. Combine apricots, water and muslin bag in large saucepan. Bring to boil, simmer, covered, for about 25 minutes, stirring occasionally, or until mixture is pulpy. Discard muslin bag.

Stir in sugar and reserved juice, stir over heat, without boiling, until sugar is dissolved. Stir in vinegar, mint and ginger. Bring to boil, simmer, uncovered, without stirring, for about 45 minutes or until conserve jells when tested. Pour into hot sterilised jars; seal when cold.

Makes about 8 cups.

CHERRY AND APPLE JAM

2 large (400g) apples
1kg cherries
1¼ cups water
⅓ cup lemon juice
5 cups (1¼ kg) sugar, approximately

Peel, core and finely chop apples. Halve cherries, remove stones. Combine apples, cherries, water and juice in large saucepan. Bring to boil, simmer, covered, for about 15 minutes or until the cherries are soft.

Measure fruit mixture, allow 1 cup sugar to each cup of fruit mixture. Return fruit mixture and sugar to pan, stir over heat, without boiling, until sugar is dissolved. Bring to boil, boil, uncovered, without stirring, for about 30 minutes or until jam jells when tested. Pour into hot sterilised jars; seal when cold.

Makes about 5 cups.

RIGHT: Clockwise from back: Dark Plum Jam, Fruit Salad Jam, Apricot and Mint Conserve, Cherry and Apple Jam.

Table from The Country Trader

ROSE PETAL JAM

You will need about 20 pesticide-free dark red roses for this recipe.

100g rose petals
3 cups water
1½ cups sugar
1 tablespoon lemon juice
1½ tablespoons Jamsetta

Trim white or yellow section from petals. Combine petals and water in large saucepan, bring to boil, simmer, covered, for 30 minutes, strain; reserve liquid.

Combine reserved liquid, sugar, juice and Jamsetta in pan, stir over heat, without boiling, until sugar is dissolved. Bring to boil, boil, uncovered, without stirring, for about 10 minutes or until jam jells when tested. Stir in petals, pour into hot sterilised jars; seal when cold.

Makes about 2 cups.

STRAWBERRY CONSERVE

1½kg strawberries, hulled
5 cups (1¼ kg) sugar
1 cup lemon juice

Place berries in large saucepan, heat, covered, for about 5 minutes to extract some of the juice from the berries. Carefully remove berries from pan with a slotted spoon, place in bowl; reserve.

Add sugar and lemon juice to berry juice in pan, stir over heat, without boiling, until sugar is dissolved. Bring to boil, boil, uncovered, without stirring, for 20 minutes. Return berries to pan, simmer, uncovered, without stirring, further 25 minutes or until jam jells when tested. Pour jam into hot sterilised jars; seal when cold.

Makes about 6 cups.

PEAR, GINGER AND LEMON JAM

5 medium (900g) lemons
6 medium (1kg) pears, peeled, chopped
¼ cup glace ginger, chopped
1¼ litres (5 cups) water
4 cups (1kg) sugar

Slice unpeeled lemons, reserve seeds, tie seeds in a piece of muslin. Combine lemons and any juice and bag of seeds with remaining ingredients in large saucepan, stir over heat, without boiling, until sugar is dissolved. Bring to boil, simmer, uncovered, without stirring, for about 1 hour or until jam jells when tested. Discard muslin bag. Pour jam into hot sterilised jars; seal when cold.

Makes about 4 cups.

LEFT: From left: Pear, Ginger and Lemon Jam, Strawberry Conserve.
BELOW: Rose Petal Jam.

PEACH JAM

3 medium (500g) lemons
1 large (200g) apple, chopped
2 cloves
10 medium (1½kg) peaches, peeled
1 cup water
½ teaspoon ground allspice
3 cups sugar

Using vegetable peeler, remove rind thinly from lemons. Squeeze juice from lemons; you will need 2 tablespoons juice. Tie lemon rind, apple and cloves in a double piece of muslin; secure with string. Halve peaches, remove stones, chop peaches.

Combine peaches, water, reserved lemon juice and muslin bag in large saucepan. Bring to boil, simmer, covered, for about 30 minutes or until fruit is just soft. Discard muslin bag.

Stir allspice and sugar into pan, stir over heat, without boiling, until sugar is dissolved. Bring to boil, boil, uncovered, without stirring, for about 15 minutes or until jam jells when tested. Pour into hot sterilised jars; seal when cold.

Makes about 3 cups.

BLUEBERRY JAM

500g blueberries
1 tablespoon lemon juice
1 teaspoon white vinegar
2 cups sugar

Combine blueberries, juice and vinegar in large saucepan, bring to boil, simmer, covered, for about 15 minutes or until blueberries are soft. Stir in sugar, stir over heat, without boiling, until sugar is dissolved. Bring to boil, boil, uncovered, without stirring, for about 15 minutes or until jam jells when tested. Pour into hot sterilised jars; seal when cold.

Makes about 2 cups.

SPICY GREEN TOMATO AND APPLE JAM

3 large (600g) apples, peeled
5 medium (500g) green tomatoes, peeled, chopped
1 cup water
½ teaspoon ground ginger
½ teaspoon ground nutmeg
1 cinnamon stick
2½ cups sugar, approximately

Chop apples, combine with tomatoes, water, ginger, nutmeg and cinnamon in a large saucepan. Bring to boil, simmer, covered, for about 30 minutes or until fruits are soft. Discard cinnamon stick.

Measure fruit mixture, allow 1 cup sugar to each cup of fruit mixture.

Return fruit mixture and sugar to pan, stir over heat, without boiling, until sugar is dissolved. Bring to boil, boil, uncovered, without stirring, for about 15 minutes or until jam jells when tested. Pour into hot sterilised jars; seal when cold.

Makes about 3 cups.

APRICOT AND PINEAPPLE JAM

25 medium (1kg) apricots
1 small (500g) pineapple, chopped
½ cup water
2 tablespoons lemon juice
3 cups sugar

Halve apricots, discard stones, cut apricots into quarters. Combine apricots, pineapple, water and juice in large saucepan. Bring to boil, reduce heat, simmer, covered, for about 15 minutes or until fruit is just soft. Stir in sugar, stir over heat, without boiling, until sugar is dissolved. Bring to boil, boil, uncovered, without stirring, for about 15 minutes or until jam jells when tested. Pour into hot sterilised jars; seal when cold.

Makes about 4 cups.

LEFT: Clockwise from front: Apricot and Pineapple Jam, Blueberry Jam, Peach Jam, Spicy Green Tomato and Apple Jam.

Table from The Country Trader

RASPBERRY JAM

1½kg raspberries
2 tablespoons lemon juice
6 cups (1½kg) sugar
1 tablespoon Framboise

Combine raspberries and juice in large saucepan, stir gently over low heat for about 5 minutes or until raspberries are soft. Stir in sugar, stir over heat, without boiling, until sugar is dissolved. Bring to boil, boil, uncovered, without stirring, for about 10 minutes or until jam jells when tested. Stir in liqueur. Pour into hot sterilised jars; seal when cold.

Makes about 6 cups.

PLUM AND APPLE JAM

10 medium (750g) plums
4 large (800g) apples
1 tablespoon lemon juice
3½ cups water
4 cups (1kg) sugar

Halve plums, reserve stones. Peel and finely chop apples, reserve seeds. Tie plum stones and apple seeds in a piece of muslin. Combine plums, apples, juice, water and muslin bag in large saucepan. Bring to boil, simmer, covered, for about 30 minutes or until fruit is soft. Discard muslin bag,. Stir in sugar, stir over heat, without boiling, until sugar is dissolved. Bring to boil, boil, uncovered, without stirring, for about 30 minutes or until jam jells when tested. Pour into hot sterilised jars; seal when cold.

Makes about 5 cups.

PEACH AND GINGER JAM

10 medium (1½kg) peaches, peeled
2 large (400g) apples, peeled, chopped
⅓ cup glace ginger, finely chopped
2 teaspoons grated lemon rind
½ cup lemon juice
6 cups (1½kg) sugar

Cut peaches in half, discard stones. Combine peaches, apples, ginger, rind and juice in large saucepan. Bring to boil, simmer, covered, for about 30 minutes or until fruit is soft.

Stir in sugar, stir over heat, without boiling, until sugar is dissolved. Bring to boil, boil, uncovered, without stirring, for about 15 minutes or until jam jells when tested. Pour jam into hot sterilised jars. Seal when cold.

Makes about 8 cups.

RIGHT: Clockwise from front: Raspberry Jam, Plum and Apple Jam, Peach and GingerJam.

RIPE TOMATO AND PASSIONFRUIT JAM

You need about 24 passionfruit.

10 medium (1kg) tomatoes, peeled, chopped
2 large (400g) apples, peeled, chopped
1/3 cup lemon juice
2 cups passionfruit pulp
4 cups (1kg) sugar

Combine tomatoes and apples in large saucepan, cook over low heat, stirring often, for about 25 minutes or until fruit is pulpy. Stir in juice, passionfruit pulp and sugar, stir over heat, without boiling, until sugar is dissolved. Bring to boil, boil, uncovered, without stirring, for about 30 minutes or until jam jells when tested. Pour jam into hot sterilised jars; seal when cold.

Makes about 5 cups.

FROZEN BERRY JAM

Any berry can be used for this recipe.

4 large (880g) oranges
1kg frozen raspberries, thawed
4 cups (1kg) sugar
2 tablespoons Creme de Framboises
1/2 cup slivered almonds

Thickly peel oranges, cut into segments; reserve any juice; discard seeds.

Combine berries, oranges, reserved juice and sugar in large saucepan, stir gently over low heat, without boiling, until sugar is dissolved. Bring to boil, boil, uncovered, without stirring, for about 30 minutes or until jam jells when tested. Stir in liqueur and almonds, stand 10 minutes before pouring into hot sterilised jars; seal when cold.

Makes about 4 cups.

BLACKBERRY AND APPLE JAM

4 large (800g) apples
800g blackberries
1/2 cup water
4 cups (1kg) sugar, approximately

Peel, core and finely chop apples. Combine apples, berries and water in large saucepan. Bring to boil, simmer, covered, for about 30 minutes or until fruit is soft.

Measure fruit mixture, allow 3/4 cup sugar to each cup of fruit mixture.

Return fruit mixture and sugar to pan, stir over heat, without boiling, until sugar is dissolved. Bring to boil, boil, uncovered, without stirring, for about 15 minutes or until jam jells when tested. Pour into hot sterilised jars; seal when cold.

Makes about 6 cups.

RIGHT: Clockwise from back: Ripe Tomato and Passionfruit Jam, Frozen Berry Jam, Blackberry and Apple Jam.

APPLE AND GINGER JAM

2 medium (360g) lemons
6 large (1¼kg) apples, peeled, sliced
1¼ litres (5 cups) water
50g fresh ginger, peeled, sliced
5 cups (1¼kg) sugar, approximately
⅔ cup glace ginger, chopped

Remove rind thinly from 1 lemon, using vegetable peeler; squeeze juice from lemons; you need ¼ cup juice.

Combine apples, water and juice in large saucepan. Tie rind and fresh ginger in a piece of muslin, add bag to pan. Bring apple mixture to boil, simmer, covered, for 30 minutes; discard muslin bag.

Measure fruit mixture, allow 1 cup sugar to each cup of fruit mixture.

Return fruit mixture and sugar to pan, stir over heat, without boiling, until sugar is dissolved. Bring to boil, boil, uncovered, without stirring, for about 15 minutes or until jam jells when tested. Stir in glace ginger; stand 5 minutes. Pour into hot sterilised jars; seal when cold.

Makes about 5 cups.

APPLE AND APRICOT JAM

18 medium (750g) apricots
5 large (1kg) apples, peeled, chopped
3 cups water
4 cups (1kg) sugar, approximately

Halve apricots and discard stones. Combine apricots, apples and water in large saucepan. Bring to boil, simmer, covered, for 30 minutes.

Measure fruit mixture, allow ¾ cup sugar to each cup of fruit mixture.

Return fruit mixture and sugar to pan, stir over heat, without boiling, until sugar is dissolved. Bring to boil, boil, uncovered, without stirring, for about 30 minutes or until jam jells when tested. Pour into hot sterilised jars; seal when cold.

Makes about 6 cups.

APPLE AND FIG JAM

3 large (600g) apples, peeled, chopped
1 litre (4 cups) water
6 medium (500g) figs, chopped
2 cups water, extra
4 cups (1kg) sugar, approximately

Combine apples and water in large saucepan, bring to boil, simmer, covered, for about 30 minutes. Stir in figs and extra water, bring to boil, simmer, covered, for 10 minutes or until figs are soft.

Measure fruit mixture, allow ¾ cup sugar to each cup of fruit mixture.

Return fruit mixture and sugar to pan, stir over heat, without boiling, until sugar is dissolved. Bring to boil, boil, uncovered, without stirring, for about 30 minutes or until jam jells when tested. Pour into hot sterilised jars; seal when cold.

Makes about 5 cups.

PINEAPPLE AND PEAR JAM

10 medium (1½kg) pears, peeled, chopped
1 large (1½kg) pineapple, chopped
1 tablespoon grated lemon rind
1⅓ cups lemon juice
2 cups water
6 cups (1½kg) sugar

Combine pears with pineapple, rind, juice and water in large saucepan. Bring to boil, simmer, uncovered, for about 45 minutes or until mixture is reduced by half.

Stir in sugar, stir over heat, without boiling, until sugar is dissolved. Bring to boil, boil, uncovered, without stirring, for about 15 minutes or until jam jells when tested. Pour jam into hot sterilised jars; seal when cold.

Makes about 8 cups.

LEFT: From left: Apple and Ginger Jam, Apple and Apricot Jam, Apple and Fig Jam. BELOW: Pineapple and Pear Jam.

Below: Serving ware from Clay Things

APPLE AND RASPBERRY JAM

3 large (600g) apples
800g raspberries
¾ cup water
4 cups (1kg) sugar, approximately
⅓ cup lemon juice
¼ cup Creme de Framboises

Peel, core and finely chop apples. Combine apples, berries and water in large saucepan, bring to boil, simmer, covered, for 1 hour.

Measure fruit mixture, allow ¾ cup sugar to each cup of fruit mixture. Return fruit mixture and sugar to pan, stir in juice, stir over heat, without boiling, until sugar is dissolved. Bring to boil, boil, uncovered, without stirring, for about 15 minutes or until jam jells when tested.

Stir in liqueur. Pour into hot sterilised jars; seal when cold.

Makes about 4 cups.

APRICOT JAM

25 medium (1kg) apricots
1½ cups water
5 cups (1¼ kg) sugar, approximately

Halve apricots and discard stones. Combine apricots and water in large saucepan, bring to boil, simmer, covered, for about 15 minutes or until apricots are soft.

Measure fruit mixture, allow 1 cup sugar to each cup of fruit mixture.

Return fruit mixture and sugar to pan, stir over heat, without boiling, until sugar is dissolved. Bring to boil, boil, uncovered, without stirring, for about 15 minutes or until jam jells when tested. Pour into hot sterilised jars; seal when cold.

Makes about 5 cups.

TRIBERRY JAM

500g strawberries, hulled
500g blackberries
500g raspberries
5 cups (1¼ kg) sugar, approximately
¼ cup lemon juice

Combine berries in large saucepan, stir gently over low heat for 5 minutes.

Measure fruit mixture, allow 1 cup sugar to each cup of fruit mixture.

Return fruit mixture and sugar to pan, stir in juice, stir over heat, without boiling, until sugar is dissolved. Bring to boil, boil, uncovered, without stirring, for about 20 minutes or until jam jells when tested. Pour jam into hot sterilised jars; seal when cold.

Makes about 5 cups.

FIG AND GINGER CONSERVE

12 medium (1kg) figs, chopped
½ cup orange juice
2 tablespoons lemon juice
1 tablespoon sweet sherry
1½ tablespoons grated fresh ginger
2 cups sugar

Combine figs, juices, sherry and ginger in large saucepan. Bring to boil, simmer, covered, for about 20 minutes or until figs are soft.

Stir in sugar, stir over heat, without boiling, until sugar is dissolved. Bring to boil, boil, uncovered, without stirring, for about 20 minutes or until conserve jells when tested. Pour into hot sterilised jars; seal when cold.

Makes about 3 cups.

LEFT: Clockwise from front: Triberry Jam, Apricot Jam, Apple and Raspberry Jam, Fig and Ginger Conserve.

Table and board from The Country Trader, basket and screen from Corso de Fiori

DRIED APRICOT JAM

500g dried apricots
1¼ litres (5 cups) water
4 cups (1kg) sugar
2 tablespoons lemon juice

Combine apricots and water in bowl; stand overnight.

Bring apricot mixture to boil in large saucepan, boil, covered, for about 15 minutes or until apricots are soft. Stir in sugar and juice, stir over heat, without boiling, until sugar is dissolved. Bring to boil, boil, without stirring, for about 30 minutes or until jam jells when tested. Pour jam into hot sterilised jars; seal when cold.

Makes about 4 cups.

PINEAPPLE JAM

2 medium (2kg) pineapples, chopped
1¼ litres (5 cups) water
⅔ cup lemon juice
6 cups (1½kg) sugar

Combine pineapples, water and juice in large saucepan. Bring to boil, simmer, covered, for about 1 hour or until pineapples are soft.

Stir in sugar, stir over heat, without boiling, until sugar is dissolved. Bring to boil, boil, uncovered, without stirring, for about 30 minutes or until jam jells when tested. Pour jam into hot sterilised jars; seal when cold.

Makes about 6 cups.

NECTARINE LIQUEUR JAM

8 large (1½kg) nectarines
½ cup lemon juice
2 cups sugar, approximately
2 tablespoons Amaretto

Halve nectarines, discard stones, finely chop nectarines. Combine nectarines and juice in large saucepan, bring to boil, simmer, covered, for about 20 minutes or until nectarines are soft.

Measure fruit mixture, allow ¾ cup sugar to each cup of fruit mixture.

Return fruit mixture and sugar to pan, stir over heat, without boiling, until sugar is dissolved. Bring to boil, boil, uncovered, without stirring, for about 10 minutes or until jam jells when tested. Stir in liqueur. Pour jam into hot sterilised jars; seal when cold.

Makes about 3 cups.

RIGHT: From left: Dried Apricot Jam, Nectarine Liqueur Jam, Pineapple Jam.

China from Shop 3, Balmain; bowl from Accoutrement; table from Corso de Fiori

REDCURRANT ORANGE JAM

1½kg redcurrants
2 tablespoons grated orange rind
1½ cups orange juice
6 cups(1½kg) sugar

Discard stems from currants, wash currants; drain. Combine currants, rind and juice in large saucepan, bring to boil, simmer, covered, for about 20 minutes or until currants are soft.

Stir in sugar, stir over heat, without boiling, until sugar is dissolved. Bring to boil, boil, uncovered, without stirring, for about 25 minutes or until jam jells when tested. Pour jam into hot sterilised jars; seal when cold.

Makes about 8 cups.

RHUBARB JAM

1½kg rhubarb, chopped
1 cup water
2 tablespoons lemon juice
5cm piece fresh ginger, peeled
5 cups (1¼kg) castor sugar, approximately
½ cup finely chopped glace ginger

Combine rhubarb, water, juice and fresh ginger in large saucepan. Bring to boil, simmer, covered, for 1 hour. Remove and discard ginger.

Measure fruit mixture, allow ¾ cup sugar to each cup of fruit mixture.

Return fruit mixture and sugar to pan, stir over heat, without boiling, until sugar is dissolved. Stir in glace ginger, bring to boil, boil, uncovered, without stirring, for about 15 minutes or until jam jells when tested. Pour jam into hot sterilised jars; seal when cold.

Makes about 6 cups.

PEACH AND PASSIONFRUIT JAM

You will need about 9 passionfruit.
4 large (800g) peaches
½ cup lemon juice
½ cup water
2½ cups sugar, approximately
¾ cup passionfruit pulp
2 tablespoons peach liqueur

Peel and halve peaches, discard stones; chop peaches finely. Combine peaches, juice and water in large saucepan, bring to boil, simmer, covered, for about 20 minutes or until peaches are soft.

Measure fruit mixture, allow ¾ cup sugar to each cup of fruit mixture.

Return fruit mixture and sugar to pan, stir over heat, without boiling, until sugar is dissolved. Bring to boil, boil, uncovered, without stirring, for about 10 minutes or until jam jells when tested. Stir in passionfruit and liqueur. Stand 10 minutes, stirring occasionally, before pouring jam into hot sterilised jars; seal when cold.

Makes about 3 cups.

RHUBARB AND ORANGE CONSERVE

2kg rhubarb, chopped
6 cups (1½kg) sugar
4 large (880g) oranges
2 medium (170g) limes
¼ cup currants
¼ cup pine nuts
2 tablespoons Cointreau

Combine rhubarb and sugar in large saucepan. Peel oranges thinly, using vegetable peeler; cut rind into thin strips. Squeeze juice from oranges (you will need 1 cup juice). Peel limes thinly, cut rind into thin strips; squeeze juice from limes (you will need 2 tablespoons juice).

Stir juices and rind into pan, stir over heat, without boiling, until sugar is dissolved. Bring to boil, boil, uncovered, without stirring, for about 45 minutes or until conserve jells when tested. Stir in currants, pine nuts and liqueur, stand 10 minutes, before pouring into hot sterilised jars; seal when cold.

Makes about 8 cups.

ABOVE: Rhubarb Jam.
RIGHT: Clockwise from front: Redcurrant Orange Jam, Peach and Passionfruit Jam, Rhubarb and Orange Conserve.

Above: Tub from The Parterre Garden

GOLDEN PLUM CONSERVE

We used greengage plums in this recipe.
14 medium (1kg) plums
1 cup water
2 tablespoons lemon juice
¼ cup orange juice
5 cups (1¼kg) sugar, approximately
1½ cups (240g) sultanas
¼ cup glace ginger, chopped
1 tablespoon rum

Halve plums, discard stones, cut plums into quarters. Combine plums, water and juices in large saucepan. Bring to boil, simmer, covered, for about 10 minutes or until plums are soft.

Measure fruit mixture, allow 1 cup sugar to each cup of fruit mixture.

Return fruit mixture and sugar to pan, stir over heat, without boiling, until sugar is dissolved. Stir in sultanas and ginger. Bring to boil, boil, uncovered, for about 20 minutes, without stirring, or until conserve jells when tested. Stir in rum. Pour into hot sterilised jars; seal when cold.

Makes about 5 cups.

QUINCE JAM

9 medium (2kg) quinces
2 litres (8 cups) water
1 tablespoon grated lemon rind
⅔ cup lemon juice
6 cups (1½kg) sugar

Peel and quarter quinces; remove and discard cores. Chop quinces into small pieces, combine with water, rind and juice in large saucepan. Bring to boil, simmer, covered, for 1 hour.

Stir in sugar, stir over heat, without boiling, until sugar is dissolved. Bring to boil, boil, uncovered, without stirring, for about 30 minutes or until jam jells when tested. Pour jam into hot sterilised jars; seal when cold.

Makes about 10 cups.

RHUBARB AND CARROT CONSERVE

4 medium (500g) carrots, chopped
500g rhubarb, chopped
1 teaspoon grated lemon rind
2 tablespoons lemon juice
1 litre (4 cups) water
4 cups (1kg) sugar
¼ cup glace ginger, chopped

Combine carrots, rhubarb, rind, juice, and water in large saucepan. Bring to boil, simmer, covered, for about 15 minutes or until carrots are soft. Stir in sugar and ginger, stir over heat, without boiling, until sugar is dissolved. Bring to boil, boil, uncovered, without stirring, for about 15 minutes or until conserve jells when tested. Pour into hot sterilised jars; seal when cold.

Makes about 4 cups.

LEFT: From left, Quince Jam, Golden Plum Conserve.
BELOW: Rhubarb and Carrot Conserve.

Below: Plate from Accoutrement, table from Corso de Fiori

MARMALADES

Marmalades are jams which always include a citrus fruit and usually have rind suspended in the mixture. Citrus fruits are rich in pectin, so there is rarely any trouble getting these jams to set. Be sure you read our tips for success on pages 2 to 5 before you start.

CUMQUAT MARMALADE

1kg cumquats
1¼ litres (5 cups) water
2 tablespoons lemon juice
5 cups (1¼ kg) sugar

Cut cumquats in half, remove seeds, tie seeds in piece of muslin. Slice cumquats thinly, place into large bowl with muslin bag and water, cover, stand overnight.

Transfer mixture to large saucepan, stir in juice. Bring to boil, simmer, covered, for about 30 minutes or until cumquat skins are soft; discard muslin bag. Add sugar, stir over heat, without boiling, until sugar is dissolved. Bring to boil, boil, uncovered, without stirring, for about 20 minutes or until marmalade jells when tested. Pour into hot sterilised jars; seal when cold.

Makes about 7 cups.

PINEAPPLE AND LEMON MARMALADE

2 medium (2kg) pineapples, peeled
8 cups (2kg) sugar
4 medium (720g) lemons
2 litres (8 cups) water

Halve pineapples, remove and reserve cores, slice flesh finely. Place flesh in large bowl, sprinkle with 2 cups of the sugar; cover, stand overnight.

Slice unpeeled lemons finely, reserve seeds. Tie reserved seeds and chopped pineapple cores in piece of muslin. Combine lemon, muslin bag and water in large saucepan. Bring to boil, simmer, uncovered, for about 40 minutes or until rind is soft and liquid is reduced by half. Discard muslin bag.

Stir in pineapple mixture and remaining sugar, stir over heat, without boiling, until sugar is dissolved. Bring to boil, boil, uncovered, without stirring, for about 20 minutes or until marmalade jells when tested. Pour into hot sterilised jars; seal when cold.

Makes about 8 cups.

MANDARIN MARMALADE

12 medium (1¼ kg) mandarins
1½ litres (6 cups) water
7 cups (1¾ kg) sugar, approximately
⅓ cup lemon juice
¼ cup Cointreau

Peel mandarins, cut rind into fine strips. Remove pith and seeds from mandarins; tie seeds in piece of muslin. Finely chop flesh. Combine rind, muslin bag, flesh and water in bowl, cover, stand overnight.

Transfer mixture to large saucepan, bring to boil, simmer, covered, for about 30 minutes or until rind is soft. Discard muslin bag.

Measure fruit mixture, allow 1 cup sugar to each cup of fruit mixture. Return fruit mixture and sugar to pan, stir over heat, without boiling, until sugar is dissolved; stir in juice. Bring to boil, boil, uncovered, without stirring, for about 35 minutes or until mixture jells when tested. Stir in liqueur, stand 10 minutes before pouring marmalade into hot sterilised jars; seal when cold.

Makes about 7 cups.

THREE FRUIT MARMALADE

4 large (880g) oranges
2 medium (360g) lemons
1 medium (390g) grapefruit
1¼ litres (5 cups) water
6 cups (1½ kg) sugar, approximately

Cut unpeeled fruit in half, cut halves into thin slices. Remove seeds, tie in piece of muslin. Combine fruit, muslin bag and water in bowl, cover, stand overnight.

Transfer mixture to large saucepan, bring to boil, simmer, covered, for about 1 hour or until rind is soft; discard bag.

Measure fruit mixture, return to pan, add ¾ cup sugar to each cup of fruit mixture. Stir over heat, without boiling, until sugar is dissolved. Bring to boil, boil, uncovered, without stirring, for about 40 minutes or until marmalade jells when tested. Pour into hot sterilised jars; seal when cold.

Makes about 7 cups.

GRAPEFRUIT AND GINGER MARMALADE

2 medium (360g) lemons
2 medium (780g) grapefruit
6cm piece fresh ginger, peeled
2½ litres (10 cups) water
1 teaspoon tartaric acid
8 cups (2kg) sugar
1 cup (165g) finely chopped glace ginger

Peel lemons, chop rind roughly, chop flesh roughly, reserve seeds and juice. Peel grapefruit, chop rind into fine strips, reserve. Chop grapefruit flesh roughly, reserve seeds and juice.

Combine lemon and grapefruit flesh with reserved juice in large saucepan. Tie reserved seeds, lemon rind and fresh ginger in a piece of muslin, add to pan.

Add grapefruit rind with water and acid.

Bring to boil, boil, uncovered, for about 1½ hours or until rind is soft and mixture has reduced by half. Discard bag.

Add sugar, stir over heat, without boiling, until sugar is dissolved; stir in glace ginger. Bring to boil, boil, uncovered, without stirring, for about 15 minutes or until marmalade jells when tested. Pour into hot sterilised jars; seal when cold.

Makes about 8 cups.

RIGHT: Clockwise from back left: Grapefruit and Ginger Marmalade, Pineapple and Lemon Marmalade, Cumquat Marmalade, Mandarin Marmalade, Three Fruit Marmalade.

China from Shop 3, Balmain; linen place mat from Cameo Antiques

LEMON AND LIME MARMALADE

3 medium (540g) lemons
5 medium (425g) limes
2 litres (8 cups) water
7 cups (1¾kg) sugar, approximately
2 tablespoons Cointreau

Remove rind from fruit, cut into thin strips. Remove and reserve pith, chop flesh roughly, reserve seeds. Combine rind, flesh and water in large saucepan. Tie pith and seeds in a piece of muslin, add to pan. Bring to boil, simmer, covered, for about 1 hour or until rind is soft. Discard bag.

Measure fruit mixture, allow ¾ cup sugar to each cup of fruit mixture. Return fruit mixture and sugar to pan, stir over heat, without boiling, until sugar is dissolved. Bring to boil, boil, uncovered, without stirring, for about 20 minutes or until marmalade jells when tested; stir in liqueur. Pour into hot sterilised jars; seal when cold.

Makes about 7 cups.

SWEET ORANGE MARMALADE

5 large (1kg) oranges
2 teaspoons citric acid
1¼ litres (5 cups) water
5 cups (1¼ kg) sugar
2 tablespoons lemon juice

Cut oranges into quarters. Using sharp knife, remove pith and rind from each quarter, reserve half the pith, discard remaining pith. Cut orange flesh into thin slices, place into a bowl, reserve seeds. Cut rind into very thin strips, place into bowl with orange flesh, add half the water, cover, stand overnight.

Tie reserved seeds and pith in piece of muslin, place bag into separate bowl with citric acid and remaining water; cover, stand overnight.

Combine contents of bowls with juice in large saucepan. Bring to boil, simmer, covered, for about 40 minutes or until rind is soft. Discard muslin bag.

Add sugar, stir over heat, without boiling, until sugar is dissolved. Bring to boil, boil, uncovered, without stirring, for about 15 minutes or until marmalade jells when tested. Pour into hot sterilised jars; seal when cold.

Makes about 7 cups.

GRAPEFRUIT MARMALADE

3 medium (1kg) grapefruit
2 medium (360g) lemons
2½ litres (10 cups) water
10 cups (2½ kg) sugar, approximately

Cut unpeeled fruit in halves, cut halves into thin slices, discard seeds. Combine fruit and water in large bowl, cover, stand overnight.

Place fruit mixture in large saucepan, bring to boil, simmer, covered, for about 45 minutes or until rind is soft.

Measure fruit mixture, allow 1 cup sugar to each cup of fruit mixture. Return fruit mixture to pan, add sugar, stir over heat, without boiling, until sugar is dissolved. Bring to boil, boil, uncovered, without stirring, for about 15 minutes or until marmalade jells when tested. Pour into hot sterilised jars; seal when cold.

Makes about 10 cups.

ABOVE: Lemon and Lime Marmalade.
RIGHT: From back: Grapefruit Marmalade, Sweet Orange Marmalade.

Right: Pot with lid from Shop 3, Balmain; plant from Sherringham's Nursery. Above: Plate from China Doll; marmalade pot from Village Living

The

ORANGE AND APRICOT MARMALADE

3 large (750g) oranges
1 cup dried apricots, chopped
2 litres (8 cups) water
8 cups (2kg) sugar, approximately

Cut unpeeled oranges in quarters, slice thinly. Place oranges and apricots in large bowl, add water, cover, stand overnight.

Place fruit mixture in large saucepan, bring to boil, simmer, covered, for about 45 minutes or until rind is soft.

Measure fruit mixture, allow 1 cup sugar to each cup of fruit mixture. Add sugar, stir over heat, without boiling, until sugar is dissolved. Bring to boil, boil, uncovered, without stirring, for about 40 minutes or until marmalade jells when tested. Pour marmalade into hot sterilised jars; seal when cold.

Makes about 8 cups.

CHUNKY BREAKFAST MARMALADE

4 large (800g) Seville oranges
2 medium (360g) lemons
1½ litres (6 cups) water
6 cups (1½kg) sugar

Cut unpeeled fruit into quarters, reserve centre pith. Cut each quarter into thick slices, reserve seeds.

Tie reserved seeds and reserved pith in a piece of muslin. Combine fruit, muslin bag and water in large bowl, cover, stand overnight.

Transfer mixture to large saucepan, bring to boil, simmer, covered, for about 1½ hours or until rind is soft. Discard muslin bag. Add sugar, stir over heat, without boiling, until sugar is dissolved. Bring to boil, boil, uncovered, without stirring, for about 10 minutes or until marmalade jells when tested. Pour into hot sterilised jars; seal when cold.

Makes about 8 cups.

RIGHT: From left: Chunky Breakfast Marmalade, Orange and Apricot Marmalade.
Bowl, spoon and napkin from Cameo Antiques

Orange
and Apricot
Marmalade

SEVILLE ORANGE MARMALADE

6 small (1kg) Seville oranges
2 litres (8 cups) water
8 cups (2kg) sugar, approximately

Slice unpeeled oranges finely, reserve seeds. Combine oranges and the water in bowl, cover; stand overnight. Place seeds in cup, barely cover with water, cover; stand overnight.

Transfer fruit mixture to large saucepan, bring to boil, simmer, covered, for about 45 minutes or until rind is soft.

Measure fruit mixture, allow 1 cup sugar to each cup of fruit mixture. Return fruit mixture and sugar to pan, stir in liquid from seeds; discard seeds. Stir over heat, without boiling, until sugar is dissolved. Bring to boil, boil, uncovered, without stirring, for about 20 minutes or until marmalade jells when tested. Pour into hot sterilised jars; seal when cold.

Makes about 12 cups.

MANDARIN JELLY MARMALADE

1 medium (390g) grapefruit
2 medium (360g) lemons
7 medium (735g) mandarins
3 litres (12 cups) water
5 cups (1¼kg) sugar, approximately
1 tablespoon Grand Marnier

Chop unpeeled grapefruit and unpeeled lemons; reserve seeds.

Peel mandarins, reserve rind and pith, chop flesh. Cut rind into thin strips, barely cover with water in bowl; reserve.

Combine grapefruit, lemons, reserved seeds, mandarin flesh and the water in large saucepan. Bring to boil, simmer, uncovered, for about 1 hour or until rind is soft. Strain mixture through fine cloth, allow liquid to drip through cloth slowly, do not squeeze cloth.

Measure liquid, pour into pan. Drain reserved mandarin rind, add to pan, bring to boil, simmer, covered, for about 15 minutes or until rind is soft. Add ¾ cup sugar to each cup of liquid. Stir over heat, without boiling, until sugar is dissolved. Bring to boil, boil, uncovered, without stirring, for about 30 minutes or until mixture jells when tested. Stir in liqueur. Pour into hot sterilised jars; seal when cold.

Makes about 4 cups.

LEFT: Mandarin Jelly Marmalade.
BELOW: Seville Orange Marmalade.
Caneware from Keyhole Furniture; china from Wedgwood

TOMATO MARMALADE

2 large (440g) oranges
10 medium (1kg) tomatoes, peeled, chopped
2 cups water
4 cups (1kg) sugar, approximately

Slice unpeeled oranges thinly, discard seeds. Combine oranges, tomatoes and water in bowl, cover; stand overnight.

Transfer mixture to large saucepan, bring to boil, simmer, covered, for about 30 minutes or until rind is soft.

Measure fruit mixture, allow ¾ cup sugar to each cup of fruit mixture. Return fruit mixture and sugar to pan, stir over heat, without boiling, until sugar is dissolved. Bring to boil, boil, uncovered, without stirring, for about 15 minutes or until marmalade jells when tested. Pour into hot sterilised jars; seal when cold.

Makes about 5 cups.

TANGY LEMON MARMALADE

6 medium (1kg) lemons
1¾ litres (7 cups) water
4 cups (1kg) sugar

Cut rind thinly from lemons, slice finely. Cut pith from lemons; chop roughly, reserve. Cut flesh into thin slices; reserve seeds.Combine flesh and rind in large bowl with water. Tie reserved pith and seeds in piece of muslin, add to bowl, cover; stand overnight.

Transfer mixture to large saucepan, bring to boil, simmer, covered, for about 40 minutes or until rind is soft. Discard muslin bag, add sugar, stir over heat, without boiling, until sugar is dissolved. Bring to boil, boil, uncovered, without stirring, for about 30 minutes or until marmalade jells when tested. Pour into hot sterilised jars; seal when cold.

Makes about 6 cups.

CARROT AND ORANGE MARMALADE

6 large (1¼kg) oranges
2 medium (360g) lemons
1 litre (4 cups) water
6 medium (700g) carrots, grated
8 cups (2kg) sugar, approximately

Slice unpeeled fruit finely; reserve seeds, tie in a piece of muslin. Combine fruit, muslin bag and water in large saucepan. Bring to boil, simmer, covered, for about 1 hour or until rind is soft. Stir in carrots, simmer 15 minutes.

Measure fruit mixture, allow ¾ cup sugar to each cup of fruit mixture. Return fruit mixture and sugar to pan, stir over heat, without boiling, until sugar is dissolved. Bring to boil, boil, uncovered, without stirring, for about 20 minutes or until marmalade jells when tested. Pour into hot sterilised jars; seal when cold.

Makes about 8 cups.

LEFT: Tomato Marmalade.
ABOVE: From left: Tangy Lemon Marmalade, Carrot and Orange Marmalade.

Left: China from Shop 3, Balmain; platter from Corso di Fiori. Above: China from Shop 3, Balmain.

FIVE FRUIT MARMALADE

1 medium (390g) grapefruit
7 medium (735g) mandarins
1 small (130g) lemon
2 large (400g) apples
2 medium (300g) pears
3 litres (12 cups) water
10 cups (2½ kg) sugar, approximately

Cut unpeeled fruit in half, slice halves thinly, remove seeds, tie in piece of muslin. Combine fruit, muslin bag and water in large bowl, cover; stand overnight.

Transfer mixture to large saucepan, bring to boil, simmer, covered, for about 1 hour or until rind is soft. Discard bag.

Measure fruit mixture, allow ¾ cup sugar to each cup of fruit mixture. Return fruit mixture and sugar to pan, stir over heat, without boiling, until sugar is dissolved. Bring to boil, boil, uncovered, without stirring, for about 40 minutes or until marmalade jells when tested. Pour into hot sterilised jars; seal when cold.

Makes about 10 cups.

THREE FRUIT JELLY MARMALADE

2 large (440g) oranges
3 medium (315g) mandarins
1 medium (180g) lemon
2 litres (8 cups) water
2½ cups sugar, approximately

Remove rind thinly from 1 orange, 1 mandarin and the lemon, cut rind into strips. Combine rind with 2 cups of the water in saucepan, bring to boil, simmer, covered, for about 30 minutes or until rind is soft. Drain, reserve liquid and rind separately.

Chop peeled and unpeeled fruit finely, combine with remaining water and reserved liquid in large saucepan. Bring to boil, simmer, covered, for about 1 hour or until fruit is soft. Strain mixture through fine cloth, allow liquid to drip through cloth slowly, do not squeeze cloth.

Measure liquid, allow 1 cup sugar to each cup of liquid, return liquid and sugar to pan, stir over heat, without boiling, until sugar is dissolved; stir in reserved rind. Bring to boil, boil, uncovered, without stirring, for about 10 minutes or until marmalade jells when tested. Pour into hot sterilised jars; seal when cold.

Makes about 3 cups.

LIME MARMALADE

12 medium (1kg) limes
1½ litres (6 cups) water
7 cups (1¾ kg) sugar, approximately

Slice unpeeled limes thinly, discard seeds. Combine limes and water in bowl, cover, stand overnight.

Transfer mixture to large saucepan, bring to boil, simmer, covered, for about 1 hour or until rind is soft.

Measure fruit mixture, allow 1 cup sugar to each cup of fruit mixture. Return fruit mixture and sugar to pan, stir over heat, without boiling, until sugar is dissolved. Bring to boil, boil, uncovered, without stirring, for about 20 minutes or until marmalade jells when tested. Pour into hot sterilised jars; seal when cold.

Makes about 9 cups.

ABOVE: Five Fruit Marmalade.
RIGHT: From back: Three Fruit Jelly Marmalade, Lime Marmalade.

Above: Bowl from The Country Trader; background cabinet from Oldentime Antiques and Old Wares

DARK WHISKY MARMALADE

5 large (1kg) oranges
2 medium (360g) lemons
2½ litres (10 cups) water
2½ cups sugar, approximately
2½ cups brown sugar, firmly packed, approximately
2 tablespoons treacle
2 tablespoons whisky

Peel oranges and lemons thickly, cut rind into thick slices, chop flesh roughly; discard seeds. Combine rind, flesh and water in large saucepan, bring to boil, simmer, covered, for about 1 hour or until the rind is soft.

Measure fruit mixture, allow ⅓ cup each sugar to each cup of fruit mixture. Return fruit mixture with sugar and treacle to pan, stir over heat, without boiling, until sugar is dissolved. Bring to boil, boil, uncovered, without stirring, for about 25 minutes or until marmalade jells when tested. Stir in whisky, pour into hot sterilised jars; seal when cold.

Makes about 5 cups.

GOLDEN ORANGE AND VEGETABLE MARMALADE

4 large (880g) oranges
1 medium (180g) lemon
2 medium (240g) carrots, grated
1 large (200g) apple, peeled, grated
3 litres (12 cups) water
1 medium (280g) cucumber, peeled, seeded
5 cups (1¼kg) sugar

Peel oranges and lemon thickly, place rind in large bowl, barely cover with water, cover, stand overnight.

Drain rind, discard water. Remove pith from rind; discard pith.

Slice rind and flesh thinly; discard seeds. Combine rind and flesh with carrots, apple and the water in large saucepan.

Grate cucumber, add to pan, bring to boil, simmer, covered, for about 2 hours or until fruit and vegetables are pulpy. Stir in sugar, stir over heat, without boiling, until sugar is dissolved. Bring to boil, boil, uncovered, without stirring, for about 20 minutes or until marmalade jells when tested. Pour into hot sterilised jars; seal when cold.

Makes about 6 cups.

RIGHT: Back: Golden Orange and Vegetable Marmalade; front: Dark Whisky Marmalade.

JELLIES

The good thing about making jelly is that you do minimal preparation. Just chop the unpeeled fruit and use the lot - skins, cores and all! Each jelly will need a simple pectin test to determine how much sugar to add; see page 2 to 5.

GRAPE JELLY

1½kg black grapes
⅔ cup water
⅓ cup lemon juice
2¼ cups sugar, approximately
1 pouch (20g) Gelfix

Using scissors, snip grapes from main stems, leaving small stems attached to grapes. Crush grapes in large saucepan, stir in water and juice. Bring to boil, simmer, covered, for about 10 minutes or until grapes are pulpy.

Strain mixture through fine cloth. Allow mixture to drip through cloth slowly, do not squeeze cloth; discard pulp.

Measure liquid, pour into large saucepan. Add correct amount of sugar (according to pectin test) to each cup of liquid. Stir over heat, without boiling, until sugar is dissolved. Bring to boil, stir in Gelfix, boil, uncovered, for about 5 minutes or until jelly sets when tested. Pour into hot sterilised jars; seal when cold.

Makes about 3 cups.

BRANDIED MULBERRY JELLY

2 large (400g) apples, chopped
1 medium lemon, chopped
1¼ litres (5 cups) water
1kg mulberries
3¾ cups sugar, approximately
2 tablespoons brandy

Combine apples, lemon and water in large saucepan. Bring to boil, simmer, covered, for 1½ hours. Stir in mulberries, simmer, covered, for about 1 hour or until berries are soft.

Strain mixture through fine cloth. Allow liquid to drip through cloth slowly, do not squeeze cloth; discard pulp.

Measure liquid, pour into large saucepan. Add correct amount of sugar (according to pectin test) to each cup of liquid, stir over heat, without boiling, until sugar is dissolved. Bring to boil, boil, uncovered, for about 15 minutes or until jelly sets when tested. Stir in brandy. Pour into hot sterilised jars; seal when cold.

Makes about 4 cups.

RASPBERRY JELLY

2kg raspberries
4 cups (1kg) sugar, approximately
1 tablespoon lemon juice

Place raspberries in large saucepan, stir over low heat for about 10 minutes or until pulpy. Strain mixture through fine cloth. Allow liquid to drip through cloth slowly, do not squeeze cloth; discard pulp.

Measure liquid, pour into large saucepan. Add correct amount of sugar (according to pectin test) to each cup of liquid, add juice, stir over heat, without boiling, until sugar is dissolved. Bring to boil, boil, uncovered, for about 10 minutes or until jelly sets when tested. Pour into hot sterilised jars; seal when cold.

Makes about 4 cups.

QUINCE JELLY

6 large (1¾kg) quinces, chopped
1¾ litres (7cups) water
5 cups (1¼kg) sugar, approximately
½ cup lemon juice

Combine quinces and water in large saucepan, bring to boil, simmer, covered, for about 1 hour or until quinces are soft.

Strain mixture through fine cloth. Allow liquid to drip through cloth slowly, do not squeeze cloth; discard pulp.

Measure liquid, pour into large saucepan. Add correct amount of sugar (according to pectin test) to each cup of liquid. Stir over heat, without boiling, until sugar is dissolved. Stir in juice, bring to boil, boil, uncovered, for about 25 minutes or until jelly sets when tested. Pour into hot sterilised jars; seal when cold.

Makes about 4 cups.

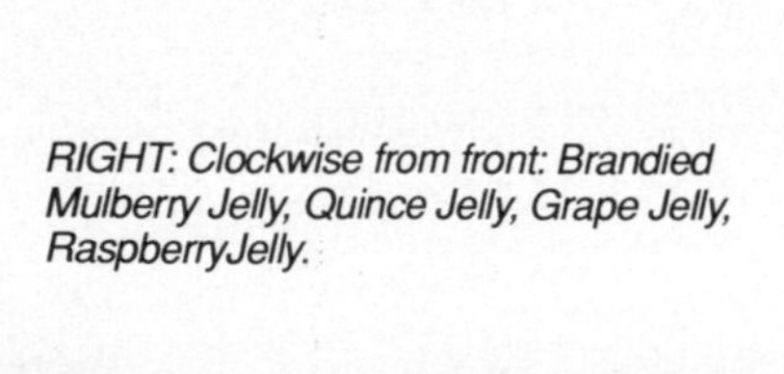

RIGHT: Clockwise from front: Brandied Mulberry Jelly, Quince Jelly, Grape Jelly, RaspberryJelly.

la Chartreuse
ERNES
Contrôlée
(GIRONDE)
AU CHATEAU

HONEY SAUTERNES JELLY

5 large (1kg) apples, chopped
2 tablespoons lemon juice
2 cups water
1 cup sauternes
1/4 cup honey
3 cups sugar, approximately

Combine apples, juice, water, wine and honey in large saucepan. Bring to boil, simmer, covered, for 1 hour.

Strain mixture through fine cloth. Allow liquid to drip through cloth slowly, do not squeeze cloth; discard pulp.

Measure liquid, pour into large saucepan. Add correct amount of sugar (according to pectin test) to each cup of liquid. Stir over heat, without boiling, until sugar is dissolved. Bring to boil, boil, uncovered, for about 10 minutes or until jelly sets when tested. Pour into hot sterilised jars; seal when cold.

Makes about 3 cups.

GRAPE AND SHERRY JELLY

1kg white grapes, crushed
1/2 cup sweet white wine
3/4 cup water
2 large (400g) apples, chopped
1 medium lemon, sliced
1 cinnamon stick
4 cardamom seeds, crushed
1 3/4 cups sugar, approximately
2 tablespoons sweet sherry

Combine grapes, wine, water, apples, lemon, cinnamon and cardamom in large saucepan. Bring to boil, simmer, covered, for 1 hour.

Strain mixture through fine cloth. Allow liquid to drip through cloth slowly, do not squeeze cloth; discard pulp.

Measure liquid, pour into large saucepan. Add correct amount of sugar (according to pectin test) to each cup of liquid. Stir over heat, without boiling, until sugar is dissolved. Bring to boil, boil, uncovered, for about 10 minutes or until jelly sets when tested; stir in sherry. Pour into hot sterilised jars; seal when cold.

Makes about 2 cups.

LEFT: Honey Sauternes Jelly.
ABOVE RIGHT: From top: Grape and Sherry Jelly, Blackberry, Apple and Mint Jelly.
Above right: Tray and napkins from China Doll

BLACKBERRY, APPLE AND MINT JELLY

2 large (400g) apples, chopped
1 medium lemon, chopped
750g blackberries
1 litre (4 cups) water
1/4 cup chopped fresh mint
2 cups sugar, approximately
1/2 teaspoon chopped fresh mint, extra

Combine apples, lemon, blackberries, water and mint in large saucepan. Bring to boil, simmer, covered, for 1 hour.

Strain mixture through fine cloth. Allow liquid to drip through cloth slowly, do not squeeze cloth; discard pulp.

Measure liquid, pour into large saucepan. Add correct amount of sugar (according to pectin test) to each cup of liquid. Stir over heat, without boiling, until sugar is dissolved. Bring to boil, boil, uncovered, for about 10 minutes or until jelly sets when tested; add extra mint. Pour into sterilised jars; seal when cold.

Makes about 2 cups.

TANGERINE JELLY

5 large (1kg) tangerines, chopped
1 medium lemon, chopped
2½ litres (10 cups) water
2½ cups sugar, approximately

Combine tangerines, lemon and water in large saucepan. Bring to boil, simmer, covered, for about 1 hour or until fruit is soft and pulpy.

Strain mixture through fine cloth. Allow liquid to drip through cloth slowly, do not squeeze cloth; discard pulp.

Measure liquid, pour into large saucepan. Add correct amount of sugar (according to pectin test) to each cup of liquid. Stir over heat, without boiling, until sugar is dissolved. Bring to boil, boil, uncovered, for about 5 minutes or until jelly sets when tested. Pour into hot sterilised jars; seal when cold.

Makes about 2 cups.

PLUM JELLY

28 medium (2kg) blood plums, chopped
1 litre (4 cups) water
⅓ cup lemon juice
3 cups sugar, approximately

Combine plums, water and juice in large saucepan. Bring to boil, simmer, covered, for about 10 minutes or until plums are soft and pulpy.

Strain mixture through fine cloth. Allow liquid to drip through cloth slowly, do not squeeze cloth; discard pulp.

Measure liquid, pour into large saucepan. Add correct amount of sugar (according to pectin test) to each cup of liquid. Stir over heat, without boiling, until sugar is dissolved. Bring to boil, boil, uncovered, for about 15 minutes or until jelly sets when tested. Pour into hot sterilised jars; seal when cold.

Makes about 3 cups.

GUAVA JELLY

13 medium (1½kg) guavas, chopped
1 litre (4 cups) water
2 cups sugar, approximately
2 tablespoons lime juice

Combine guavas and water in large saucepan. Bring to boil, simmer, covered, for about 25 minutes or until guavas are soft and pulpy.

Strain mixture through fine cloth. Allow liquid to drip through cloth slowly, do not squeeze cloth; discard pulp.

Measure liquid, pour into large saucepan. Add correct amount of sugar (according to pectin test) to each cup of liquid. Stir over heat, without boiling, until sugar is dissolved. Add juice, bring to boil, boil, uncovered, for about 15 minutes or until jelly sets when tested. Pour into hot sterilised jars; seal when cold.

Makes about 2 cups.

BELOW: Tangerine Jelly.
RIGHT: From top: Plum Jelly, Guava Jelly.
Below: Window from A.J.Healy; lace from Oldentime Antiques and Old Wares. Right: China and roses from Whitehouse Interiors

REDCURRANT JELLY

1½kg redcurrants
1½ litres (6 cups) water
1 teaspoon lemon juice
2½ cups sugar, approximately
1 tablespoon Grand Marnier

Combine redcurrants, water and juice in large saucepan, bring to boil, simmer, covered, for about 30 minutes or until currants are soft.

Strain mixture through fine cloth. Allow liquid to drip through cloth slowly, do not squeeze cloth; discard pulp.

Measure liquid, pour into large saucepan. Add correct amount of sugar (according to pectin test) to each cup of liquid. Stir over heat, without boiling, until sugar is dissolved. Bring to boil, boil, uncovered, for about 15 minutes or until jelly sets when tested. Stir in liqueur, pour into hot sterilised jars; seal when cold.

Makes about 3 cups.

LEFT: Redcurrant Jelly.
Basket and saucepan from Sydney Antique Centre; tea-towel from The Bay Tree

PASSIONFRUIT JELLY

18 medium (1kg) passionfruit
1¼ litres (5 cups) water
2 cups sugar, approximately
⅔ cup lemon juice

Wash and dry passionfruit, remove pulp. You will need 1¾ cups of pulp.

Combine pulp, skins and water in large saucepan. Bring to boil, simmer, covered, for about 25 minutes or until the insides of the skins are tender.

Strain mixture through fine cloth. Allow liquid to drip through cloth slowly, do not squeeze cloth; discard skins and pulp.

Measure liquid, pour into large saucepan. Add correct amount of sugar (according to pectin test) to each cup of liquid. Stir in juice, stir over heat, without boiling, until sugar is dissolved. Bring to boil, boil, uncovered, for about 10 minutes or until jelly sets when tested. Pour into hot sterilised jars; seal when cold.

Makes about 2 cups.

REDCURRANT AND RASPBERRY JELLY

600g redcurrants
800g raspberries
1 cup water
2 cups sugar, approximately

Combine fruit and water in large saucepan. Bring to boil, simmer, covered, for about 25 minutes or until fruit is soft.

Strain mixture through fine cloth. Allow liquid to drip through cloth slowly, do not squeeze cloth; discard pulp.

Measure liquid, pour into large saucepan. Add correct amount of sugar (according to pectin test) to each cup of liquid. Stir over heat, without boiling, until sugar is dissolved. Bring to boil, boil, uncovered, for about 10 minutes or until jelly sets when tested. Pour into hot sterilised jars; seal when cold.

Makes about 2 cups.

BLACKBERRY JELLY

1kg blackberries
2 cups water
3 cups sugar, approximately
⅔ cup lemon juice

Combine berries and water in large saucepan. Bring to boil, simmer, covered, for about 25 minutes or until berries are soft and pulpy.

Strain mixture through fine cloth. Allow liquid to drip through cloth slowly, do not squeeze cloth; discard pulp.

Measure liquid, pour into large saucepan. Add correct amount of sugar (according to pectin test) to each cup of liquid. Stir in juice, stir over heat, without boiling, until sugar is dissolved. Bring to boil, boil, uncovered, for about 20 minutes or until jelly sets when tested. Pour into hot sterilised jars; seal when cold.

Makes about 3 cups.

APPLE JELLY

5 medium (1kg) apples, chopped
1½ litres (6 cups) water
4 cups (1kg) sugar, approximately

Combine apples and water in large saucepan, bring to boil, simmer, covered, for 1 hour.

Strain mixture through fine cloth. Allow liquid to drip through cloth slowly, do not squeeze cloth; discard pulp.

Measure liquid, pour into large saucepan. Add correct amount of sugar (according to pectin test) to each cup of liquid. Stir over heat, without boiling, until sugar is dissolved. Bring to boil, boil, uncovered, for about 15 minutes or until jelly sets when tested. Pour into hot sterilised jars; seal when cold.

Makes about 3 cups.

LEFT: From left: Passionfruit Jelly, Redcurrant and Raspberry Jelly.
ABOVE: From left: Blackberry Jelly, Apple Jelly.

Above: Plate and ceramic dish from Shop 3, Balmain; tiles from Country Floors

CHUTNEYS

A condiment of Indian origin, chutney is a kind of tangy sweet pickle usually served as an accompaniment to curries, hot and cold meats and savouries. There are many varieties, all based on chopped fruit and/or vegetables, sugar and vinegar. Not much can go wrong as mixtures are simply cooked until thick. Once you have opened a jar, keep, covered, in the refrigerator. For best results, be sure to read our tips for success on pages 2 to 5 before you start.

GRAPE AND APPLE CHUTNEY

1kg seedless white grapes, halved
4 large (800g) apples, peeled, chopped
1 cup chopped raisins
1 cup cider vinegar
½ teaspoon grated lemon rind
½ cup lemon juice
½ teaspoon ground allspice
½ teaspoon ground cloves
½ teaspoon ground ginger
¼ teaspoon ground cinnamon
½ teaspoon salt
¼ teaspoon paprika
3 cups brown sugar, firmly packed

Combine grapes, apples, raisins, vinegar, rind, juice, spices, salt and paprika in large saucepan. Bring to boil, simmer, uncovered, for about 1 hour, stirring occasionally, or until fruit is soft.

Add sugar, stir over heat, without boiling, until sugar is dissolved. Bring to boil, simmer, uncovered, for about 30 minutes, stirring occasionally, or until thick. Pour into hot sterilised jars; seal when cold.

Makes about 7 cups.

RHUBARB CHUTNEY

1kg rhubarb, chopped
2 medium (240g) onions, chopped
3 cups brown sugar, firmly packed
1½ cups (240g) sultanas
2½ cups white vinegar
1 tablespoon white mustard seeds
1 teaspoon mixed spice
1 teaspoon ground ginger

Combine all ingredients in large saucepan, bring to boil, simmer, uncovered, stirring occasionally, for about 1¼ hours or until mixture is thick. Pour into hot sterilised jars; seal when cold.

Makes about 5 cups.

APRICOT AND ORANGE CHUTNEY

4 cups (500g) dried apricots, chopped
1 litre (4 cups) water
1¼ cups white vinegar
¾ cup sultanas
1 clove garlic, crushed
1 tablespoon grated orange rind
⅓ cup orange juice
3 black peppercorns
1 cup sugar

Combine apricots, water, vinegar, sultanas, garlic, rind, juice and peppercorns in large saucepan. Bring to boil, simmer, uncovered, for about 30 minutes or until apricots are pulpy.

Add sugar, stir over heat, without boiling, until sugar is dissolved. Bring to boil, boil, uncovered, for 5 minutes. Pour into hot sterilised jars; seal when cold.

Makes about 4 cups.

RIGHT: Clockwise from front: Rhubarb Chutney, Grape and Apple Chutney, Apricot and Orange Chutney.

Tray from Polain Interiors

PEAR AND WALNUT CHUTNEY

10 medium (1½kg) pears, peeled
2 large (400g) apples, peeled
1 cup white vinegar
¾ cup lemon juice
1 cup brown sugar, firmly packed
1 cup chopped raisins
1 cup chopped dates
1 cup chopped walnuts

Chop pears and apples, combine with remaining ingredients in large saucepan. Bring to boil, simmer gently, uncovered, stirring occasionally, for about 1¼ hours or until mixture is thick. Pour into hot sterilised jars; seal when cold.

Makes about 5 cups.

APPLE AND TOMATO CHUTNEY

2 large (400g) apples, peeled, chopped
20 medium (2kg) ripe tomatoes, peeled, chopped
2 large (240g) onions, chopped
1½ cups raw sugar
1¼ litres (5 cups) brown vinegar
2 teaspoons ground ginger
½ teaspoon ground cinnamon
½ teaspoon ground cloves

Combine all ingredients in large saucepan. Stir over heat, without boiling, until sugar is dissolved. Bring to boil, simmer, uncovered, stirring occasionally, for about 1½ hours or until mixture is thick. Pour chutney into hot sterilised jars; seal when cold.

Makes about 7 cups.

BANANA CHUTNEY

7 medium (1kg) bananas, chopped
3 cups (500g) dates, chopped
1 teaspoon grated fresh ginger
1 medium (120g) onion, chopped
2 teaspoons grated lemon rind
¼ cup lemon juice
2 cups brown vinegar
1 cup brown sugar, firmly packed
2 teaspoons curry powder

Combine bananas, dates, ginger, onion, rind, juice and vinegar in large saucepan. Bring to boil, simmer, uncovered, for about 20 minutes or until fruit is soft. Stir in sugar and curry powder, stir over heat, without boiling, until sugar is dissolved. Bring to boil, simmer, uncovered, stirring occasionally, for about 20 minutes or until mixture is thick. Pour into hot sterilised jars; seal when cold.

Makes about 5 cups.

RIGHT: Clockwise from left: Banana Chutney, Apple and Tomato Chutney, Pear and Walnut Chutney.

SPICY TOMATO CHUTNEY

10 medium (1kg) ripe tomatoes, peeled, chopped
2 large (400g) apples, peeled, chopped
2 medium (240g) onions, chopped
1½ cups brown vinegar
1 cup brown sugar, firmly packed
¼ teaspoon chilli powder
½ teaspoon dry mustard
¾ cup sultanas
1 clove garlic, crushed
2 teaspoons curry powder
2 teaspoons ground allspice

Combine all ingredients in large saucepan, stir over heat, without boiling, until sugar is dissolved. Bring to boil, simmer, uncovered, stirring occasionally, for about 1 hour or until mixture is thick. Pour into hot sterilised jars; seal when cold.

Makes about 6 cups.

APPLE AND RED PEPPER CHUTNEY

2 large (400g) apples, peeled, chopped
3 medium (500g) red peppers, chopped
2 medium (240g) onions, chopped
2 cloves garlic, crushed
½ cup currants
2 cups cider vinegar
½ cup dry white wine
2½ cups water
2 teaspoons black peppercorns
1 teaspoon cloves
1½ cups brown sugar, firmly packed

Combine apples, peppers, onions, garlic, currants, vinegar, wine and water in large saucepan. Tie peppercorns and cloves in piece of muslin; add to pan. Bring to boil, simmer, uncovered, stirring occasionally, for about 15 minutes or until apples and peppers are soft.

Add sugar, stir over heat, without boiling, until sugar is dissolved. Bring to boil, simmer, stirring occasionally, for about 1½ hours or until thick. Discard muslin bag. Pour mixture into hot sterilised jars; seal when cold.

Makes about 3 cups.

BELOW: Spicy Tomato Chutney.
RIGHT: Apple and Red Pepper Chutney.
Below: Bowl from Villa Italiana. Right: Jar from Appley Hoare Antiques

DRIED APRICOT CHUTNEY

1¾ litres (7 cups) water
6 cups (780g) dried apricots
4 medium (480g) onions, chopped
1 cup sultanas
2½ cups brown sugar, firmly packed
1 tablespoon white mustard seeds
3 small fresh red chillies, chopped
2 cups brown vinegar
2 teaspoons grated orange rind
1 tablespoon orange juice
1 teaspoon ground coriander
1 teaspoon ground cumin
½ cup chopped pecans or walnuts

Combine water and apricots in large bowl, cover, stand overnight.

Combine undrained apricot mixture, onions, sultanas, sugar, seeds, chillies, vinegar, rind, juice and spices in large saucepan. Stir over heat, without boiling, until sugar is dissolved. Bring to boil, simmer, uncovered, stirring occasionally, for about 1½ hours or until mixture is thick. Stir in nuts. Pour chutney into hot sterilised jars; seal when cold.

Makes about 7 cups.

CHERRY CHUTNEY

1kg cherries, pitted, chopped
1 cup currants
½ cup brown sugar
2 tablespoons golden syrup
1 cup white vinegar
1¼ teaspoons ground allspice

Combine all ingredients in large saucepan. Stir over heat, without boiling, until sugar is dissolved. Bring to boil, simmer, uncovered, stirring occasionally, for about 30 minutes or until mixture is thick. Pour chutney into hot sterilised jars; seal when cold.

Makes about 3 cups.

PEARS AND SULTANA CHUTNEY

10 medium (1½kg) pears, peeled, chopped
2 large (400g) apples, chopped
1 medium (120g) onion, finely chopped
2 cups (320g) sultanas
2 tablespoons grated fresh ginger
1 clove garlic, crushed
1 teaspoon chilli powder
½ teaspoon ground cardamom
¼ teaspoon cayenne pepper
2 cinnamon sticks
1¾ cups brown sugar, firmly packed
2 cups cider vinegar
1 cup water
¼ cup orange juice

Combine all ingredients in large saucepan, stir over heat, without boiling, until sugar is dissolved. Bring to boil, simmer, uncovered, stirring occasionally, for about 2 hours or until mixture is thick. Discard cinnamon sticks. Pour into hot sterilised jars; seal when cold.

Makes about 6 cups.

APPLE AND DATE CHUTNEY

2 cups brown vinegar
1 cup brown sugar, firmly packed
1 tablespoon grated fresh ginger
2 small fresh red chillies, chopped
1 teaspoon white mustard seeds
2 cups water
3 large (600g) apples, peeled, chopped
2 cups (320g) chopped dates
2 cups (340g) chopped raisins
2 medium (240g) onions, chopped

Combine vinegar, sugar, ginger, chillies, seeds and water in large saucepan. Stir over heat, without boiling, until sugar is dissolved. Stir in apples, dates, raisins and onions. Bring to boil, simmer, uncovered, stirring occasionally, for about 1 hour or until mixture is thick. Pour into hot sterilised jars; seal when cold.

Makes about 6 cups.

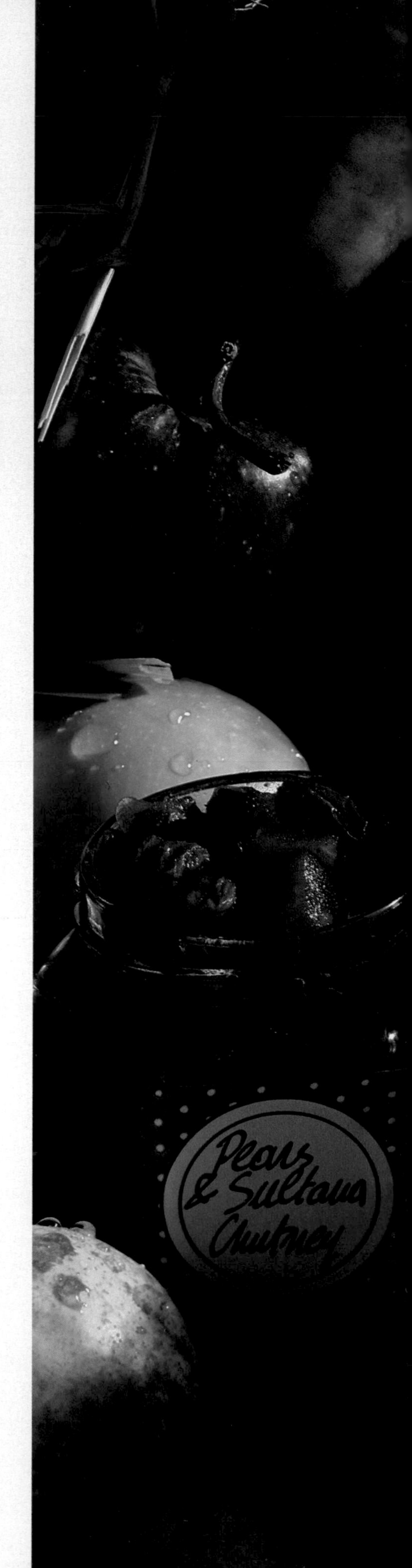

RIGHT: Clockwise from back: Dried Apricot Chutney, Cherry Chutney, Apple and Date Chutney, Pears and Sultana Chutney.
Fabric from Boyac; barrel and sign from The Country Trader

Cherry Chutney
Apple & Date Chutney

SWEET FRUIT CHUTNEY

5 large (1kg) apples, peeled, chopped
10 medium (1kg) tomatoes, peeled, chopped
4 medium (500g) onions, chopped
1½ cups (240g) sultanas
¾ cup chopped raisins
1 cup currants
1 litre (4 cups) brown vinegar
4 cups (1kg) brown sugar, firmly packed
2 teaspoons grated orange rind
2 teaspoons grated fresh ginger
2 teaspoons ground cinnamon
½ teaspoon ground cloves
pinch cayenne pepper

Combine all ingredients in large saucepan, stir over heat, without boiling, until sugar is dissolved. Bring to boil, simmer, uncovered, stirring occasionally, for about 1½ hours or until mixture is thick. Pour chutney into hot sterilised jars; seal when cold.

Makes about 6 cups.

LEFT: From left: Sweet Fruit Chutney, Dried Fruit Chutney.
ABOVE: Tamarillo Apple Chutney.

Above: China from Wedgwood

DRIED FRUIT CHUTNEY

1¼ cups (200g) chopped dried pears
1⅓ cups (200g) chopped dried apricots
1¼ cups (200g) chopped dates
2 cups (200g) chopped dried apples
1⅓ cups (200g) sultanas
1 litre (4 cups) water
2 cups cider vinegar
2 cups brown sugar, firmly packed
½ teaspoon chilli powder
½ teaspoon turmeric
½ teaspoon ground nutmeg
½ teaspoon ground ginger
1 clove garlic, crushed

Combine pears, apricots, dates, apples, sultanas and water in large bowl, cover; stand overnight.

Combine undrained fruit mixture with remaining ingredients in large saucepan. Stir over heat, without boiling, until sugar is dissolved. Bring to boil, simmer, uncovered, stirring occasionally, for about 1¼ hours or until mixture is thick. Pour into hot sterilised jars; seal when cold.

Makes about 7 cups.

TAMARILLO APPLE CHUTNEY

20 medium (1½kg) tamarillos
6 large (1¼kg) apples, peeled, chopped
4 medium (500g) onions, chopped
¾ cup sultanas
4 cups (1kg) brown sugar, firmly packed
2 cups brown vinegar
2 cups white vinegar
1 teaspoon ground allspice
1 teaspoon ground cinnamon

Cut a small cross in base of each tamarillo, drop into large saucepan of boiling water, stand 2 minutes, drain; place in cold water. Peel away skins, chop flesh finely.

Combine tamarillo flesh with remaining ingredients in large saucepan. Stir over heat, without boiling, until sugar is dissolved. Bring to boil, simmer, uncovered, stirring occasionally, for about 2 hours or until mixture is thick. Pour into hot sterilised jars; seal when cold.

Makes about 5 cups.

NECTARINE CHUTNEY

11 medium (2kg) nectarines, chopped
1 medium (150g) green pepper, chopped
2½ cups white vinegar
4 cups (1kg) brown sugar, firmly packed
1 cup chopped dates
¼ cup chopped glace ginger
1 teaspoon ground cinnamon
¼ teaspoon ground cloves
1 teaspoon grated orange rind

Combine all ingredients in large saucepan, stir over heat, without boiling, until sugar is dissolved. Bring to boil, simmer, uncovered, stirring occasionally, for about 2 hours, or until mixture is thick. Pour chutney into hot sterilised jars; seal when cold.

Makes about 6 cups.

BLACKBERRY CHUTNEY

2 large (400g) apples, peeled, chopped
2 medium (240g) onions, chopped
1kg blackberries
1½ cups brown sugar, firmly packed
2 cups brown vinegar
½ teaspoon ground allspice
½ teaspoon ground ginger

Combine all ingredients in large saucepan, stir over heat, without boiling, until sugar is dissolved. Bring to boil, simmer, uncovered, stirring occasionally, for about 1½ hours, or until mixture is thick. Pour chutney into hot sterilised jars; seal when cold.

Makes about 3 cups.

OLD-FASHIONED DATE CHUTNEY

6 medium (600g) ripe tomatoes, peeled, chopped
3 cups (500g) dates, chopped
¾ cup currants
¾ cup white vinegar
2 cups water
¼ cup brown sugar
½ teaspoon ground ginger
½ teaspoon dry mustard
¼ teaspoon mixed spice
⅓ cup chopped walnuts or pecans

Combine all ingredients in large saucepan, stir over heat, without boiling, until sugar is dissolved. Bring to boil, simmer, stirring occasionally, for about 40 minutes or until mixture is thick. Pour into hot sterilised jars; seal when cold.

Makes about 5 cups.

LEFT: From left: Nectarine Chutney, Blackberry Chutney, Old-Fashioned Date Chutney.

Chair from The Parterre Garden

APRICOT CHUTNEY

12 medium (1kg) apricots, chopped
3 medium (360g) onions, chopped
2 cups brown vinegar
1 cup sultanas
1 cup brown sugar, firmly packed
2 teaspoons grated fresh ginger
1 small fresh green chilli, chopped
½ cup brandy

Combine apricots, onions, vinegar, sultanas, sugar, ginger and chilli in large saucepan. Stir over heat, without boiling, until sugar is dissolved. Bring to boil, simmer, uncovered, stirring occasionally, for about 1½ hours or until mixture is thick. Stir in brandy, pour into hot sterilised jars; seal when cold.

Makes about 5 cups.

GREEN TOMATO CHUTNEY

10 medium (1kg) green tomatoes, chopped
2 medium (240g) onions, chopped
2 large (400g) apples, chopped
1 litre (4 cups) brown vinegar
2½ cups brown sugar, firmly packed
1½ cups (240g) sultanas
1½ teaspoons dry mustard
1 teaspoon ground cinnamon
¼ teaspoon ground cloves
¼ teaspoon cayenne pepper

Combine all ingredients in large saucepan, stir over heat, without boiling, until sugar is dissolved. Bring to boil, simmer, uncovered, stirring occasionally, for about 1½ hours or until mixture is thick. Pour chutney into hot sterilised jars; seal when cold.

Makes about 6 cups.

BEETROOT CHUTNEY

6 medium (1kg) beetroot, peeled, chopped
2 medium (240g) onions, chopped
4 large (800g) apples, peeled, chopped
2 large (440g) oranges, peeled, chopped
1 cup sugar
1 teaspoon grated lemon rind
2 tablespoons lemon juice
2 cups white vinegar
1 small fresh red chilli, chopped
1 clove garlic, crushed
1 teaspoon coriander seeds

Steam or microwave beetroot until just tender. Combine beetroot with remaining ingredients in large saucepan. Bring to boil, simmer, uncovered, stirring occasionally, for about 1 hour or until mixture is thick. Pour into hot sterilised jars; seal when cold.

Makes about 8 cups.

RIGHT: From left: Apricot Chutney, Beetroot Chutney, Green Tomato Chutney.

Beetroot Chutney
From the kitchen of:
Green Tomato

PINEAPPLE CHUTNEY

1 large (1½kg) pineapple, chopped
1 medium (120g) onion, chopped
1 cup cider vinegar
1 cup brown sugar, firmly packed
½ teaspoon grated fresh ginger
½ teaspoon chilli powder
¼ teaspoon ground cloves
½ cup dry sherry

Combine pineapple, onion, vinegar, sugar, ginger, chilli powder and cloves in large saucepan, stir over heat, without boiling, until sugar is dissolved. Bring to boil, simmer, uncovered, stirring occasionally, for about 20 minutes or until mixture is thick. Stir in sherry, pour into hot sterilised jars; seal when cold.

Makes about 3 cups.

GREEN MANGO CHUTNEY

6 medium (1½kg) green mangoes, peeled, chopped
1 tablespoon coarse cooking salt
1¾ cups sugar
2½ cups brown vinegar
¾ cup chopped dates
¾ cup chopped raisins
2 tablespoons grated fresh ginger
2 cloves garlic, crushed
1 teaspoon chilli powder
1 teaspoon ground cinnamon
1 teaspoon ground cumin

Place mangoes into large bowl, sprinkle with salt, barely cover with cold water, cover; stand overnight.

Drain mangoes, discard salt water. Combine sugar and vinegar in large saucepan, stir over heat, without boiling, until sugar is dissolved. Stir in mangoes and remaining ingredients, bring to boil, simmer, uncovered, stirring occasionally, for about 45 minutes or until mixture is thick. Pour into hot sterilised jars; seal when cold.

Makes about 8 cups.

INDIAN CHUTNEY

2 large (400g) apples, peeled, chopped
4 medium (500g) onions, chopped
3 cups (500g) dates, chopped
1 teaspoon cayenne pepper
1 teaspoon ground ginger
1 teaspoon dry mustard
1¼ litres (5 cups) white vinegar
2½ cups brown sugar, firmly packed

Combine apples, onions, dates, pepper, ginger, mustard and vinegar in large saucepan. Bring to boil, simmer, uncovered, for about 1 hour or until thick and pulpy. Add sugar, stir over heat, without boiling, until sugar is dissolved. Bring to boil, boil, uncovered, for 5 minutes. Pour into hot sterilised jars; seal when cold.

Makes about 5 cups.

MINTED APRICOT AND APPLE CHUTNEY

2 cups (300g) dried apricots, chopped
4 large (800g) apples, peeled, chopped
1 cup white vinegar
2 medium (240g) onions, chopped
2½ cups brown sugar, firmly packed
¼ cup chopped fresh mint
¾ cup sultanas

Place apricots in bowl, cover with cold water, stand overnight. Drain apricots.

Combine apricots with remaining ingredients in large saucepan, stir over heat, without boiling, until sugar is dissolved. Bring to boil, simmer, uncovered, stirring occasionally, for about 45 minutes or until mixture is thick. Pour into hot sterilised jars; seal when cold.

Makes about 6 cups.

ABOVE LEFT: Indian Chutney.
RIGHT: Clockwise from back: Minted Apricot and Apple Chutney, Green Mango Chutney, Pineapple Chutney.

Above left: Copper bowl, jug and cloth from Bengalerie

APPLE AND APRICOT CHUTNEY

2 large (400g) apples, peeled, chopped
12 medium (500g) apricots, pitted, chopped
2 medium (240g) onions, chopped
1½ cups white vinegar
½ cup chopped dates
2 teaspoons grated fresh ginger
1½ cups brown sugar, firmly packed
1 tablespoon dry mustard
2 cloves garlic, crushed
1 teaspoon black mustard seeds
½ teaspoon ground cumin
¼ teaspoon ground cardamom
½ teaspoon ground coriander

Combine all ingredients in large saucepan, stir over heat, without boiling, until sugar is dissolved. Bring to boil, simmer, uncovered, stirring occasionally, for about 1 hour or until mixture is thick. Pour into hot sterilised jars; seal when cold.

Makes about 5 cups.

COUNTRY GARDEN CHUTNEY

20 medium (1½kg) plums, pitted, chopped
3 large (600g) apples, peeled, chopped
10 medium (1kg) tomatoes, peeled, chopped
4 medium (500g) onions, chopped
1 medium (280g) green cucumber, chopped
2 litres (8 cups) brown vinegar
2 cups brown sugar, firmly packed
1½ tablespoons white mustard seeds
2 teaspoons mixed spice
6 black peppercorns
6 cloves
3 small fresh red chillies
2cm piece fresh ginger, peeled

Combine plums, apples, tomatoes, onions, cucumber, vinegar, sugar, seeds and spice in large saucepan. Tie peppercorns, cloves, chillies and ginger in piece of muslin; add to pan. Bring to boil, simmer, uncovered, stirring occasionally, for about 1½ hours or until mixture is thick.Discard bag. Pour into hot sterilised jars; seal when cold.

Makes about 10 cups.

LEMON AND MUSTARD SEED CHUTNEY

4 medium (720g) lemons
2 teaspoons coarse cooking salt
2 tablespoons white mustard seeds
2 medium (240g) onions, chopped
1 cup cider vinegar
1 teaspoon mixed spice
½ cup chopped raisins
1 cup sugar

Chop unpeeled lemons; discard seeds. Combine lemons and salt in large bowl, cover, stand overnight.

Place mustard seeds in large saucepan, stir over heat until seeds have popped. Add undrained lemon mixture, onions, vinegar, spice, raisins and sugar, stir over heat, without boiling, until sugar is dissolved. Bring to boil, simmer, uncovered, stirring occasionally, for about 45 minutes or until mixture is thick. Pour into hot sterilised jars; seal when cold.

Makes about 3 cups.

RIGHT: From back: Country Garden Chutney, Apple and Apricot Chutney, Lemon and Mustard Seed Chutney.

Chest from the Australian East India Co.

PEACH AND LEMON CHUTNEY

8 black peppercorns
4 small dried red chillies
2 cloves
1 cinnamon stick
5 medium (750g) peaches, pitted, chopped
3 medium (360g) onions, chopped
2 cups brown sugar, firmly packed
2 cups brown vinegar
1 cup sultanas
3 teaspoons grated fresh ginger
2 cloves garlic, crushed
2 teaspoons grated lemon rind
¼ cup lemon juice

Tie peppercorns, chillies, cloves and cinnamon in a piece of muslin. Combine muslin bag, peaches, onions, sugar, vinegar, sultanas, ginger, garlic, rind and juice in large saucepan. Stir over heat, without boiling, until sugar is dissolved. Bring to boil, simmer, uncovered, stirring occasionally, for about 1½ hours or until mixture is thick. Discard bag. Pour into hot sterilised jars; seal when cold.

Makes about 4 cups.

PLUM CHUTNEY

60g butter
2 cloves garlic, crushed
2 teaspoons grated fresh ginger
2 teaspoons ground cumin
1 teaspoon ground cardamom
2 teaspoons white mustard seeds
2 medium (240g) onions, sliced
14 medium (1kg) plums, pitted, chopped
2 large (400g) apples, peeled, chopped
2 cups brown sugar, firmly packed
1 cup dry red wine
2 cups white vinegar

Heat butter in large saucepan, add garlic and ginger, cook 1 minute. Stir in spices, seeds and onions, cook until onions are soft. Stir in remaining ingredients, stir over heat, without boiling, until sugar is dissolved. Bring to boil, simmer, uncovered, stirring occasionally, for about 1½ hours or until thick. Pour into hot sterilised jars; seal when cold.

Makes about 6 cups.

LEFT: From left: Peach and Lemon Chutney, Plum Chutney.
RIGHT: From back: Spiced Plum Chutney, Peach and Apple Chutney.

Right: Background chest from The Australian East India Co.

SPICED PLUM CHUTNEY

14 medium (1kg) plums, pitted, chopped
5 medium (500g) tomatoes, peeled, chopped
3 medium (360g) onions, chopped
3 medium (360g) carrots, chopped
1 large (200g) apple, peeled, chopped
1 cup chopped raisins
2 cups brown sugar, firmly packed
2 teaspoons coarse cooking salt
3½ cups brown vinegar
1 cinnamon stick
½ teaspoon cloves
3 small dried red chillies
1 star anise
1 teaspoon black peppercorns

Combine plums, tomatoes, onions, carrots, apples, raisins, sugar, salt and vinegar in large saucepan. Stir over heat without boiling, until sugar is dissolved. Tie cinnamon, cloves, chillies, star anise and peppercorns in piece of muslin. Add muslin bag to pan, bring to boil, simmer, uncovered, stirring occasionally, for about 2 hours or until mixture is thick. Discard muslin bag. Pour into hot sterilised jars; seal when cold.

Makes about 9 cups.

PEACH AND APPLE CHUTNEY

7 medium (1kg) peaches, pitted, peeled, chopped
5 large (1kg) apples, peeled, chopped
2 medium (240g) onions, chopped
1 cup chopped raisins
2 teaspoons grated fresh ginger
¾ teaspoon ground nutmeg
¾ teaspoon ground allspice
¾ teaspoon dry mustard
½ teaspoon grated orange rind
2 teaspoons grated lemon rind
1½ cups orange juice
3 cups white vinegar
2 cups sugar
2 cups brown sugar, firmly packed

Combine fruit, onions, raisins, spices, mustard, rinds, juice and vinegar in large saucepan. Bring to boil, simmer, uncovered, for about 40 minutes or until mixture is thick.

Stir in sugars, stir over heat, without boiling, until sugars are dissolved. Bring to boil, simmer, uncovered, stirring occasionally, for about 1 hour or until mixture is thick. Pour into hot sterilised jars; seal when cold.

Makes about 6 cups.

APPLE AND PRUNE CHUTNEY

5 large (1kg) apples, peeled, chopped
1 cup prunes, pitted, chopped
¼ cup lemon juice
¾ cup sugar
½ teaspoon ground nutmeg
1 cup white vinegar

Combine all ingredients in large saucepan, stir over heat, without boiling, until sugar is dissolved. Bring to boil, simmer, uncovered, stirring occasionally, for about 30 minutes or until mixture is thick. Pour chutney into hot sterilised jars; seal when cold.

Makes about 3 cups.

FEIJOA CHUTNEY

10 medium (1kg) feijoas, peeled, chopped
3 medium (360g) onions, chopped
2 cups (320g) chopped dates
2 cups (340g) chopped raisins
2 cups brown sugar, firmly packed
1 tablespoon ground ginger
½ teaspoon ground cloves
½ teaspoon cayenne pepper
1 tablespoon curry powder
3 cups white vinegar
2 cups water

Combine all ingredients in large saucepan, stir over heat, without boiling, until sugar is dissolved. Bring to boil, simmer, uncovered, stirring occasionally, for about 1½ hours or until mixture is thick. Pour chutney into hot sterilised jars; seal when cold.

Makes about 8 cups

APRICOT BANANA CHUTNEY

2 cups (300g) dried apricots, chopped
1 cup brown vinegar
2 cups water
2 teaspoons grated fresh ginger
1 tablespoon tomato paste
¼ cup golden syrup
1 small onion, chopped
¼ cup mixed peel
¼ cup sultanas
¼ teaspoon mixed spice
1 cup brown sugar, firmly packed
2 medium (300g) bananas, chopped

Combine apricots, vinegar, water, ginger, paste, syrup, onion, peel, sultanas and spice in large saucepan. Bring to boil, simmer, uncovered, stirring occasionally, for about 20 minutes or until apricots are soft. Stir in sugar and bananas, stir over heat, without boiling, until sugar is dissolved. Pour into hot sterilised jars; seal when cold.

Makes about 3 cups.

RIGHT: Clockwise from front: Apricot Banana Chutney, Apple and Prune Chutney, Feijoa Chutney.

Basket from Accoutrement

PICKLES

Pickles mostly fall into two categories: those that have a clear, sweet and/or spicy vinegar poured over various vegetables, or those that are thick and pulpy. These are thickened either by slow cooking to evaporate the liquid and concentrate the flavours, or by thickening the liquid with flour.
Generally, you need large wide-mouthed jars for the vinegar-based recipes, and vegetables are chopped to suit yourself. In these cases, we haven't specified how many cups the pickles make as it depends on the chopped size and how tightly the vegetables are packed into the jars. It is important that the ingredients are completely covered with the vinegar mixture to complete the pickling process and prevent vegetables from deteriorating. All pickles need to be refrigerated after opening. Before starting, read our hints for success on pages 2 to 5.

SPICY MUSTARD PICKLES

¼ medium (500g) cauliflower, chopped
250g green beans, chopped
3 medium (360g) onions, chopped
1 medium (150g) red pepper, chopped
¼ cup coarse cooking salt
2 tablespoons seeded mustard
2 teaspoons dry mustard
3 teaspoons curry powder
¼ teaspoon turmeric
1¾ cups white vinegar
1 cup brown sugar, firmly packed
2 tablespoons plain flour
¼ cup white vinegar, extra

Combine cauliflower, beans, onions and pepper in large bowl, sprinkle with salt, cover; stand overnight.

Rinse vegetables under cold water; drain. Combine vegetables, mustards, curry, turmeric, vinegar and sugar in large saucepan. Stir over heat, without boiling, until sugar is dissolved. Bring to boil, simmer, uncovered, for about 10 minutes or until vegetables are just tender.

Stir in blended flour and extra vinegar, stir over heat until mixture boils and thickens. Pour into hot sterilised jars; seal when cold.

Makes about 4 cups.

CHOW CHOW PICKLES

2 cups (375g) dried kidney beans
2 medium (300g) red peppers, chopped
2 medium (300g) green peppers, chopped
¼ medium (500g) cauliflower, chopped
400g green beans, chopped
1 litre (4 cups) brown vinegar
1½ cups brown sugar, firmly packed
2 tablespoons dry mustard
¼ cup white mustard seeds
2 teaspoons turmeric
310g can corn kernels, drained
¼ cup plain flour
⅓ cup water

Cover kidney beans with water in bowl, cover, stand overnight; drain.

Add beans to large saucepan of boiling water, boil, uncovered, for about 1 hour or until tender; drain.

Boil, steam or microwave peppers, cauliflower and green beans until just soft.

Combine vinegar, sugar, dry mustard, mustard seeds and turmeric in large saucepan, stir over heat, without boiling, until sugar is dissolved. Add kidney beans and vegetables with blended flour and water, stir over heat until mixture boils and thickens. Pour into hot sterilised jars; seal when cold.

Makes about 7 cups.

CURRIED GREEN TOMATO PICKLES

10 medium (1kg) green tomatoes, sliced
1 large (170g) onion, sliced
1 small (150g) green cucumber, sliced
1 stick celery, sliced
¼ cup coarse cooking salt
2 cups white vinegar
1 cup sugar
½ teaspoon cayenne pepper
2 teaspoons curry powder
2 teaspoons dry mustard
¼ cup cornflour
½ cup white vinegar, extra

Combine tomatoes, onion, cucumber and celery in bowl, sprinkle with salt, cover; stand overnight.

Rinse vegetables under cold water; drain well. Combine vinegar and sugar in large saucepan, stir over heat, without boiling, until sugar is dissolved.

Stir in vegetables, pepper, curry, mustard and blended cornflour and extra vinegar. Stir over heat until mixture boils and thickens. Spoon into hot sterilised jars; seal when cold.

Makes about 5 cups.

LEFT: Spicy Mustard Pickles.
ABOVE: From back: Chow Chow Pickles, Curried Green Tomato Pickles.
Left: Jar and table from Village Living

GHERKINS IN SPICED VINEGAR

1½ litres (6 cups) water
¾ cup coarse cooking salt
2kg gherkin cucumbers

SPICED VINEGAR
1 litre (4 cups) white vinegar
2¼ cups sugar
2 cinnamon sticks
2 teaspoons black peppercorns
2 teaspoons cloves

Combine water and salt in large saucepan, stir over heat until salt is dissolved; cool. Wash gherkins well, place in large bowl, cover gherkins completely with salt water, cover, stand 48 hours.

Drain gherkins, rinse under cold water. Pack gherkins in large sterilised jar, cover completely with spiced vinegar; seal.

Spiced Vinegar: Combine all ingredients in saucepan, stir over heat, without boiling, until sugar is dissolved. Bring to boil, simmer mixture 2 minutes, stand 5 minutes, strain; cool.

PICKLED PEPPERS

13 medium (2kg) red peppers
1 litre (4 cups) white vinegar
1 tablespoon black peppercorns
6 sprigs fresh parsley
3 sprigs fresh thyme
2 bay leaves

Cut peppers in half lengthways, remove seeds. Place peppers, skin side up, under hot grill. Grill until skin blisters, cool slightly; remove skins. Cut peppers, pack into hot sterilised jars.

Combine vinegar, peppercorns and herbs in saucepan. Bring to boil, simmer, uncovered, for 5 minutes; strain. Pour vinegar over peppers to cover completely; seal when cold.

PICKLED BABY MUSHROOMS

1 litre (4 cups) white vinegar
2 bay leaves
2 teaspoons black peppercorns
5cm piece fresh ginger, peeled
1 nutmeg
1¼kg baby mushrooms

Combine vinegar, bay leaves, peppercorns, ginger and nutmeg in large saucepan. Bring to boil, simmer, uncovered, for 15 minutes; strain.

Combine vinegar mixture and mushrooms in large saucepan, bring to boil, simmer, covered, for about 1 hour or until mushrooms are tender. Pour into hot sterilised jar; seal when cold.

LEFT: Gherkins in Spiced Vinegar.
BELOW: From left: Pickled Peppers, Pickled Baby Mushrooms.

Left: Board from The Australian East India Co.

SUGAR-FREE MIXED PICKLES

½ medium (1kg) cauliflower, chopped
2 teaspoons coarse cooking salt
I large (400g) green cucumber, chopped
1 medium (150g) green pepper, chopped
1 medium (150g) red pepper, chopped

VINEGAR
2 cups white vinegar
2 teaspoons coarse cooking salt
8 black peppercorns
1 bay leaf

Place cauliflower into colander, sprinkle with a teaspoon of the salt, cover, stand cauliflower overnight.

Add cucumber and remaining salt, stand I hour; rinse under cold water, drain.

Add vegetables to large saucepan of boiling water, boil 5 minutes or until just tender. Rinse vegetables under cold water, drain, cool. Pack vegetables into large sterilised jar, cover completely with vinegar; seal.

Vinegar: Combine all ingredients in saucepan, bring to boil, simmer, uncovered, 5 minutes; strain, cool.

SPICY MIXED PICKLES

small piece (250g) cauliflower, chopped
250g pickling onions
2 medium (240g) carrots, sliced
250g green peas

SPICED VINEGAR
2 small fresh red chillies, chopped
6 cloves
3½ cups white vinegar
¾ cup sugar

Bring large saucepan of water to boil, add vegetables, bring to boil, drain; cool. Pack vegetables into large sterilised jar, cover completely with spiced vinegar; seal.

Spiced Vinegar: Combine chillies, cloves, vinegar and sugar in saucepan. Stir over heat, without boiling, until sugar is dissolved, cool; discard cloves.

ABOVE: Sugar-Free Mixed Pickles.
RIGHT: From left: Spicy Mixed Pickles, Cucumbers in Garlic Mustard Vinegar.

Right: Cupboard from Yvonne Phillips Antiques

CUCUMBERS IN GARLIC MUSTARD VINEGAR

7 small (1kg) green cucumbers, sliced
2 tablespoons coarse cooking salt

GARLIC MUSTARD VINEGAR
¾ cup cider vinegar
½ cup white vinegar
¼ cup water
1½ tablespoons sugar
1 teaspoon white mustard seeds
2 cloves garlic, thinly sliced

Combine cucumbers and salt in large bowl, cover, stand 24 hours.

Rinse cucumbers under cold water; drain. Pack slices into large sterilised jar, cover completely with garlic mustard vinegar; seal.

Garlic Mustard Vinegar: Combine vinegars, water, sugar, seeds and garlic in saucepan. Stir over heat, without boiling, until sugar is dissolved; cool.

PICKLED ONIONS

1kg pickling onions
½ cup coarse cooking salt
1¼ litres (5 cups) water
I litre (4 cups) white vinegar
½ cup sugar
1 cinnamon stick
3cm piece fresh ginger, peeled
1 small fresh red chilli, chopped
1 teaspoon cloves
1 teaspoon black peppercorns

Combine onions, salt and water in large bowl, cover, stand overnight.

Drain onions, rinse well; pack into large sterilised jar. Combine remaining ingredients in large saucepan, stir over heat, without boiling, until sugar is dissolved. Bring to boil, simmer, uncovered, for 10 minutes; cool. Strain vinegar mixture over onions to cover completely; seal.

PICKLED BEETROOT

6 medium (1kg) beetroot
2 cups sugar
1 litre (4 cups) white vinegar
1 cup water
3 small dried red chillies
1 star anise
6 black peppercorns

Wash beetroot, cut off leafy tops, without breaking skin.

Add beetroot to large saucepan of boiling water, simmer, covered, for about 1 hour or until skins are removed easily. Cool beetroot, cut in half, pack into sterilised jar.

Combine sugar, vinegar, water, chillies, star anise and peppercorns in saucepan, stir over heat, without boiling, until sugar is dissolved; cool. Strain over beetroot to cover completely; seal.

PICCALILLI

¼ medium (500g) cauliflower, chopped
2 medium (240g) carrots, sliced
2 celery sticks, sliced
2 medium (200g) green tomatoes, chopped
1 medium (280g) green cucumber, sliced
250g pickling onions, quartered
1 cup coarse cooking salt
1¼ litres (5 cups) white vinegar
1 cup sugar
1 tablespoon turmeric
1 tablespoon dry mustard
½ teaspoon ground ginger
2 cloves garlic, crushed
2 small fresh red chillies, chopped
¼ cup cornflour
¼ cup white vinegar, extra

Combine cauliflower, carrots, celery, tomatoes, cucumber, onions and salt in large bowl, cover, stand overnight.

Rinse vegetables well under cold water; drain well.

Combine vinegar, sugar, turmeric, mustard, ginger, garlic and chillies in large saucepan. Bring to boil, add vegetables, simmer, covered, for about 5 minutes or until vegetables are just tender. Stir in blended cornflour and extra vinegar, stir until mixture boils and thickens. Pour into hot sterilised jars; seal when cold.

Makes about 12 cups.

LEFT: From left: Pickled Beetroot, Pickled Onions.
ABOVE: Piccalilli.

Above: China from Shop 3, Balmain

SPICED VEGETABLE PICKLES

2 medium (560g) green cucumbers, peeled
½ medium (1kg) cauliflower, chopped
6 medium (250g) spring onions, halved
250g green beans, chopped
1 medium (150g) red pepper, chopped
2 tablespoons coarse cooking salt

SPICED VINEGAR
1½ litres (6 cups) white vinegar
¼ cup sugar
1 tablespoon black peppercorns
2cm piece fresh ginger, peeled, sliced
5 small fresh red chillies, halved
3 bay leaves
2 cloves garlic, chopped

Cut cucumbers in half lengthways, remove seeds: chop cucumbers coarsely. Combine cucumbers, cauliflower, onions, beans and pepper in large bowl. Sprinkle with salt, cover with boiling water, stand 10 minutes; drain.

Pack vegetables into sterilised jars, cover vegetables completely with spiced vinegar; seal.

Spiced Vinegar: Combine vinegar and sugar in saucepan, stir over heat, without boiling, until sugar is dissolved. Tie remaining ingredients in a piece of muslin, add to pan. Bring to boil, cool. Discard muslin bag.

SPICED PRUNES

2⅔ cups (500g) prunes
1½ cups strained cold tea
2½ cups brown vinegar
1 cup brown sugar, firmly packed
½ cup sugar
1 cinnamon stick
1 teaspoon cloves
1 nutmeg, quartered

Combine prunes and tea in bowl, cover, stand overnight.

Transfer prune mixture to saucepan, bring to boil, simmer, uncovered, for about 10 minutes or until prunes are soft, drain; discard liquid.

Combine vinegar and sugars in large saucepan, stir over heat, without boiling, until sugars are dissolved. Tie spices in a piece of muslin, add to pan. Bring to boil, simmer, uncovered, for 10 minutes. Add prunes, simmer, uncovered, 5 minutes.

Pack prunes into hot sterilised jar. Discard muslin bag. Pour hot liquid over prunes; seal when cold.

LEFT: From back: Spiced Vegetable Pickles, Spiced Prunes.
ABOVE RIGHT: Curried Gherkin Slices.

CURRIED GHERKIN SLICES

1½kg gherkin cucumbers, sliced
1 medium (120g) onion, sliced
1 medium (150g) green pepper, sliced
¼ cup coarse cooking salt
2 cups brown vinegar
1½ cups brown sugar, firmly packed
1 tablespoon curry powder
½ teaspoon ground allspice
½ teaspoon mixed spice
¼ teaspoon ground cloves
¼ teaspoon ground cinnamon
½ teaspoon cumin seeds
½ teaspoon coriander seeds
½ teaspoon ground black pepper

Combine cucumbers, onion, pepper and salt in large bowl, cover, stand 3 hours.

Rinse well under cold water; drain well.

Combine vegetables, vinegar, sugar and spices in large saucepan. Stir over heat, without boiling, until sugar is dissolved. Bring to boil, simmer, uncovered, for 15 minutes. Pour into hot sterilised jars; seal when cold.

ABOVE : Clockwise from back: Pickled Grapes, Pickled Apples, Pickled Bananas, Orange Pickle.
RIGHT: Sugar-Free Pickled Eggplants.

PICKLED GRAPES

500g white grapes
500g black grapes
1½ cups white vinegar
¼ cup orange juice
1 teaspoon grated lemon rind
½ cup sugar
2 cinnamon sticks
½ teaspoon mixed spice
6 cloves
5cm piece fresh ginger, peeled, chopped

Wash grapes, remove stems, pack grapes into large hot sterilised jar.

Combine remaining ingredients in saucepan, stir over heat, without boiling, until sugar is dissolved. Bring to boil, simmer 2 minutes, stand 5 minutes. Strain hot liquid over grapes to cover completely; seal when cold.

ORANGE PICKLE

7 large (1½kg) oranges
1 teaspoon coarse cooking salt
2½ litres (10 cups) hot water
2 cups sugar
¼ cup golden syrup
¾ cup brown vinegar
½ cup water, extra
6 cardamom pods, bruised
¼ teaspoon black peppercorns
½ teaspoon ground cinnamon
¼ teaspoon mixed spice
¼ teaspoon ground cloves

Combine whole unpeeled oranges, salt and water in large saucepan, bring to boil, simmer, covered, for about 45 minutes or until rind is soft. Drain oranges; cool. Halve oranges, slice halves thinly.

Combine sugar, golden syrup, vinegar, extra water, cardamom, peppercorns, cinnamon, spice and cloves in large saucepan, stir over heat, without boiling, until sugar is dissolved. Bring to boil, simmer, covered, for 10 minutes; strain.

Combine sugar syrup with orange slices in pan. Bring to boil, simmer, covered, for 20 minutes, stand 5 minutes. Pack orange slices into hot sterilised jar, pour over liquid to cover completely; seal when cold.

PICKLED BANANAS

¾ cup white vinegar
1½ cups brown sugar, firmly packed
1½ teaspoons grated lemon rind
8 cloves
3 cardamom pods, bruised
½ teaspoon cracked black peppercorns
pinch saffron powder
½ teaspoon ground nutmeg
13 medium (2kg) firm bananas

Combine vinegar, sugar, rind, cloves, cardamom, peppercorns, saffron and nutmeg in large saucepan. Stir over heat, without boiling, until sugar is dissolved. Bring to boil, boil, uncovered, for 5 minutes; simmer, covered, further 5 minutes. Peel and slice bananas, pack into hot sterilised jar. Strain hot liquid into jar to cover bananas completely; seal when cold.

SUGAR-FREE PICKLED EGGPLANTS

50(1kg) baby eggplants
2 medium (240g) onions, sliced
1 clove garlic, crushed
2 teaspoons black peppercorns
2 teaspoons white mustard seeds
2 small fresh red chillies, sliced
fresh dill sprigs
1 litre (4 cups) white vinegar, approximately

Cut several slashes lengthways down each eggplant. Add eggplants to large saucepan of boiling salted water, remove from heat, stand 5 minutes; drain.

Pack eggplants and onions into large sterilised jar with garlic, peppercorns, seeds, chillies and dill. Fill jars with vinegar; seal.

PICKLED APPLES

The apples will absorb some of the liquid on standing.

3 cups sugar
2½ cups white vinegar
1 teaspoon ground cinnamon
5 large (1kg) apples, peeled, quartered

Combine sugar, vinegar and cinnamon in large saucepan. Stir over heat, without boiling, until sugar is dissolved. Add apples, bring to boil, simmer, uncovered, stirring occasionally, for about 10 minutes or until apples are just tender.

Pack apples into large hot sterilised jar, pour over vinegar mixture to cover apples completely; seal when cold.

SPICY ORANGE SEGMENTS

10 large (2kg) oranges, segmented
1 cup cider vinegar
½ cup water
2 cinnamon sticks
½ teaspoon cloves
½ cup orange juice
2 cups sugar

Layer orange segments into hot sterilised jar. Combine remaining ingredients in saucepan, stir over heat, without boiling, until sugar is dissolved. Bring to boil, simmer 1 minute, pour over orange slices to cover completely; seal when cold.

CORN PICKLE

3 medium (360g) onions, chopped
1 medium (280g) cucumber, chopped
1 medium (150g) green pepper, chopped
4 medium (400g) tomatoes, peeled, chopped
2 x 440g cans corn kernels, drained
2½ cups cider vinegar
½ cup water
1 cup sugar
2 teaspoons coarse cooking salt
2 teaspoons dry mustard
½ teaspoon turmeric
¼ cup cornflour
½ cup water, extra

Combine onions, cucumber, pepper, tomatoes, corn, vinegar, water, sugar, salt, mustard and turmeric in large saucepan. Bring to boil, simmer, covered, stirring occasionally, for 1 hour.

Stir in blended cornflour and extra water, stir over heat until mixture boils and thickens. Pour into hot sterilised jars; seal when cold.

Makes about 10 cups.

PICKLED RED CABBAGE

1 medium (4kg) red cabbage
2 tablespoons coarse cooking salt
3 cups white vinegar
2 cups water
½ cup sugar
1 tablespoon cloves
1 cinnamon stick
2 teaspoons black peppercorns
¼ teaspoon ground nutmeg
¼ teaspoon ground ginger

Remove discoloured outer leaves from cabbage, cut cabbage into quarters, remove thick core.

Shred cabbage finely, place in large bowl in layers, sprinkling between each layer with the salt, cover, stand overnight.

Drain cabbage, rinse under cold water, drain well. Pack cabbage into large sterilised jar.

Combine remaining ingredients in large saucepan, bring to boil, cool. Strain vinegar over cabbage in jar to cover completely; seal.

TOMATO AND APPLE PICKLE

10 medium (1kg) tomatoes, peeled, chopped
1 large (200g) apple, chopped
1 medium (120g) onion, chopped
3 teaspoons white mustard seeds
1 tablespoon ground ginger
3 black peppercorns
1½ cups white vinegar
1 cup brown sugar, firmly packed

Combine all ingredients in large saucepan, stir over heat, without boiling, until sugar is dissolved. Bring to boil, simmer, uncovered, stirring occasionally, for about 45 minutes or until mixture is thick. Pour pickle mixture into hot sterilised jars; seal when cold.

Makes about 4 cups.

LEFT: Clockwise from back: Spicy Orange Segments, Pickled Red Cabbage, Corn Pickle.
BELOW: Tomato and Apple Pickle.

RELISHES

Sharp, tangy relishes are based on fruit and/or vegetables and usually contain vinegar and sugar, but generally not in large enough quantities to preserve the ingredients for as long as most other pickles. Relishes must be kept in the refrigerator and will keep for about a month. They add zest to hot or cold meats, curries and savoury snacks. Be sure to read our hints for success on pages 2 to 5 before you start.

CORN RELISH

3 x 440g cans corn kernels, drained
2 medium (240g) onions, chopped
1 medium (150g) red pepper, chopped
1 medium (150g) green pepper, chopped
2 celery sticks, chopped
2 cups cider vinegar
1¾ cups white vinegar
1 cup sugar
1 tablespoon dry mustard
1 tablespoon white mustard seeds
1 teaspoon turmeric
½ teaspoon ground cloves
¼ cup cornflour
¼ cup white vinegar, extra

Combine corn, onions, peppers, celery, vinegars, sugar, mustard, seeds, turmeric and cloves in large saucepan. Bring to boil, simmer, uncovered, for about 45 minutes, stirring occasionally, or until mixture thickens slightly. Stir in blended cornflour and extra vinegar, stir until mixture boils and thickens. Pour into hot sterilised jars; seal when cold.

Makes about 6 cups.

SPICY GREEN TOMATO RELISH

10 medium (1kg) green tomatoes, sliced
1 medium (120g) onion, sliced
1kg gherkin cucumbers, chopped
1 medium (150g) green pepper, chopped
½ cup coarse cooking salt
2 cups cider vinegar
1 cup white vinegar
1 teaspoon dry mustard
½ teaspoon ground allspice
¼ teaspoon mixed spice
¼ teaspoon ground cinnamon
¼ teaspoon ground black pepper
1 cup brown sugar, firmly packed

Combine vegetables in large bowl, sprinkle with salt, cover, stand several hours, rinse under cold water; drain well.

Combine vegetables, vinegars and spices in large saucepan. Bring to boil, simmer, uncovered, stirring occasionally, for about 45 minutes or until vegetables are pulpy. Stir in sugar, stir over heat, without boiling, until sugar is dissolved. Bring to boil, boil, uncovered, for 15 minutes. Pour into hot sterilised jars; seal when cold.

Makes about 5 cups.

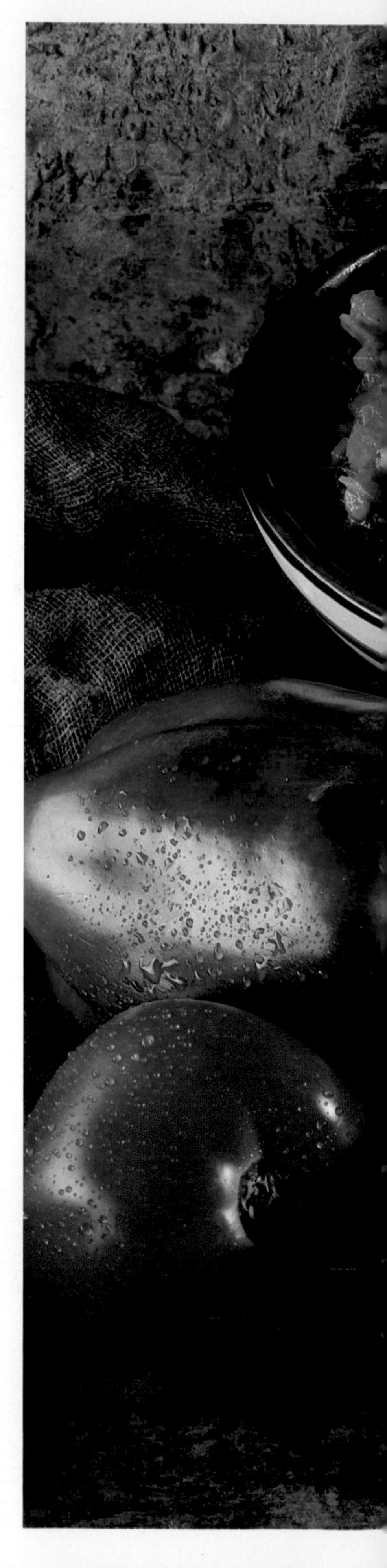

RIGHT: From back: Spicy Green Tomato Relish, Corn Relish.
Bowls from Villa Italiana

PAREK

PATTY'S TOMATO RELISH

15 medium (1½kg) ripe tomatoes, peeled, chopped
3 medium (360g) onions, chopped
1½ cups brown vinegar
1½ cups brown sugar, firmly packed
1½ tablespoons dry mustard
1 tablespoon curry powder
½ teaspoon cayenne pepper
2 teaspoons coarse cooking salt

Combine all ingredients in large saucepan, bring to boil, simmer, uncovered, stirring occasionally, for about 1¼ hours or until mixture is pulpy. Pour into hot sterilised jars; seal when cold.

Makes about 4 cups.

LEFT: From back: Patty's Tomato Relish, Prune Relish.
BELOW: Papaw and Chilli Relish.
Left: Basket, knife from The Australian East India Co.

PRUNE RELISH

2⅔ cup (500g) pitted prunes, chopped
2½ cups clear apple juice
20g butter
1 small (75g) onion, chopped
1 tablespoon dry mustard
1 tablespoon cider vinegar
2 tablespoons brandy

Combine prunes and juice in bowl, cover, stand overnight.

Melt butter in saucepan, add onion, cook until soft. Stir in prune mixture, mustard, vinegar and brandy, bring to boil, simmer, uncovered, for about 25 minutes, stirring occasionally, or until mixture is thick and pulpy. Pour into hot sterilised jars; seal when cold.

Makes about 4 cups.

PAPAW AND CHILLI RELISH

½ teaspoon black peppercorns
½ teaspoon pimentos
1 medium (1½kg) papaw, chopped
2 large (400g) apples, peeled, chopped
4 medium (400g) tomatoes, peeled, chopped
2 cups sugar
3 cups white vinegar
2 teaspoons coarse cooking salt
3 small fresh red chillies, chopped
2 teaspoons grated fresh ginger

Tie peppercorns and pimentos in piece of muslin, combine with remaining ingredients in large saucepan.

Stir over heat, without boiling, until sugar is dissolved. Bring to boil, simmer, uncovered, stirring occasionally, for about 1½ hours or until mixture is thick; discard muslin bag. Pour into hot sterilised jars; seal when cold.

Makes about 5 cups.

PROCESSOR MINT RELISH

3 medium (500g) onions, chopped
4 large (800g) apples, peeled, chopped
2 medium (300g) green peppers, chopped
8 medium (800g) ripe tomatoes, peeled, chopped
2 cups fresh mint leaves, tightly packed
¾ cup chopped dates
1 tablespoon grated fresh ginger
2 teaspoons white mustard seeds
2½ cups white vinegar
1¼ cups sugar

Combine onions, apples, peppers, tomatoes and mint in bowl. Blend or process mixture in batches until chopped.

Transfer mixture to large saucepan, add dates, ginger, seeds, vinegar and sugar. Stir over heat, without boiling, until sugar is dissolved. Bring to boil, simmer, uncovered, stirring occasionally, for about 1 hour or until mixture is thick. Pour mixture into hot sterilised jars; seal when cold.

Makes about 8 cups.

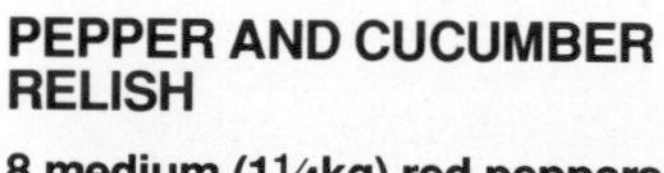

PEPPER AND CUCUMBER RELISH

8 medium (1¼kg) red peppers, chopped
8 medium (1¼kg) green peppers, chopped
3 small fresh red chillies, chopped
6 medium (720g) onions, chopped
6 medium (600g) ripe tomatoes, chopped
4 medium (1¼kg) green cucumbers, chopped
1 tablespoon white mustard seeds
1½ cups white vinegar
1½ cups water
1½ cups sugar
1 teaspoon ground cinnamon
2 tablespoons cornflour
¼ cup water, extra

Combine peppers, chillies, onions, tomatoes and cucumbers in large saucepan. Stir in seeds, vinegar, water, sugar and cinnamon. Stir over heat, without boiling, until sugar is dissolved.

Bring to boil, simmer, uncovered, stirring occasionally, for about 1½ hours or until mixture is thick. Stir in blended cornflour and extra water, stir until mixture boils and thickens. Pour into hot sterilised jars; seal when cold.

Makes about 8 cups.

ZUCCHINI AND APPLE RELISH

5 medium (750g) zucchini, grated
1½ tablespoons coarse cooking salt
3 large (600g) apples, peeled, chopped
4 medium (500g) onions, chopped
2 cups brown vinegar
1½ cups (250g) raisins, chopped
¾ cup brown sugar
½ teaspoon garam masala
½ teaspoon ground coriander

Place zucchini in colander, sprinkle with salt, stand 2 hours, rinse under cold water; drain on absorbent paper.

Combine zucchini, apples, onions, vinegar and raisins in large saucepan. Bring to boil, simmer, covered, for about 20 minutes or until mixture is pulpy. Stir in sugar and spices, stir over heat until sugar is dissolved. Bring to boil, simmer, uncovered, stirring occasionally, for about 20 minutes or until mixture is thick. Pour into hot sterilised jars; seal when cold.

Makes about 6 cups.

LEFT: From left: Pepper and Cucumber Relish, Processor Mint Relish.
RIGHT: Zucchini and Apple Relish.

Left: Knife from The Australian East India Co.

GREEN TOMATO RELISH

10 medium (1kg) green tomatoes, chopped
1 large (170g) onion, chopped
1 cup cider vinegar
¾ cup sugar
2 teaspoons dry mustard
1 teaspoon curry powder
1 teaspoon turmeric
¼ teaspoon chilli powder
1 tablespoon cornflour
1 tablespoon cider vinegar, extra

Combine tomatoes, onion, vinegar, sugar, mustard, curry powder, turmeric and chilli in large saucepan. Bring to boil, simmer, covered, for about 40 minutes or until mixture is pulpy.

Stir in blended cornflour and extra vinegar, stir until mixture boils and thickens. Pour into hot sterilised jars; seal when cold.

Makes about 3 cups.

ORIENTAL RELISH

1 medium (180g) lemon
1 large (220g) orange
1 medium (120g) onion, grated
2 x 425g cans tomatoes
3 large (600g) apples, peeled, chopped
1 cinnamon stick
2 star anise
2 tablespoons grated fresh ginger
1 teaspoon ground allspice
½ teaspoon cardamom seeds
1½ cups brown sugar, firmly packed
¾ cup brown vinegar
1 cup water

Chop unpeeled lemon and orange; discard seeds. Blend or process lemon and orange until almost smooth. Combine lemon mixture, onion, undrained crushed tomatoes and remaining ingredients in large saucepan. Stir over heat, without boiling, until sugar is dissolved. Bring to boil, simmer, uncovered, stirring occasionally, for about 1½ hours or until mixture is thick. Discard cinnamon sticks and star anise. Pour into hot sterilised jars; seal when cold.

Makes about 7 cups

SWEET AND SOUR RELISH

1 medium (1kg) pineapple, chopped
2 teaspoons coarse cooking salt
1 litre (4 cups) brown vinegar
1 tablespoon grated fresh ginger
2 cloves garlic, crushed
2 large (340g) onions, chopped
1 medium (150g) red pepper, chopped
1 tablespoon tomato paste
2 cups water
1½ cups sugar

Place pineapple in large bowl, sprinkle with salt, cover, stand overnight.

Rinse pineapple, discard liquid. Combine pineapple, vinegar, ginger, garlic, onions, pepper, paste and water in large saucepan. Bring to boil, simmer, uncovered, for 30 minutes. Add sugar, stir over heat, without boiling, until sugar is dissolved. Bring to boil, simmer, uncovered, stirring occasionally, for about 30 minutes or until mixture is thick. Pour into hot sterilised jars; seal when cold.

Makes about 4 cups.

LEFT: Sweet and Sour Relish.
ABOVE: From front: Green Tomato Relish, Oriental Relish.

Left :Glass and jar from The Australian East India Co. Above: Glass bowl and plate from Shop 3, Balmain; table from Corso de Fiori

BLACKBERRY RELISH

1kg blackberries
½ cup water
1 tablespoon sugar
1 teaspoon dry mustard
1 teaspoon ground allspice
½ teaspoon ground cinnamon
1 cup brown vinegar

Combine half the blackberries and the water in large saucepan. Bring to boil, simmer, covered, for about 10 minutes or until berries are soft. Blend or process mixture until smooth, return to pan.

Stir in remaining berries and remaining ingredients, bring to boil, simmer, uncovered, stirring occasionally, for about 15 minutes or until mixture is thick. Pour into hot sterilised jars; seal when cold.

Makes about 4 cups.

APRICOT RELISH

25 medium (1kg) apricots
2 medium (240g) onions, finely chopped
1 tablespoon grated fresh ginger
½ cup sultanas
1 cup sugar
2 teaspoons French mustard
½ teaspoon ground cinnamon
2 cups cider vinegar

Halve apricots, discard stones. Combine apricots with remaining ingredients in large saucepan. Stir over heat, without boiling, until sugar is dissolved. Bring to boil, simmer, uncovered, stirring occasionally, for about 1½ hours or until mixture is thick. Pour into hot sterilised jars; seal when cold.

Makes about 4 cups.

PEPPER RELISH

3 medium (450g) red peppers
3 medium (450g) green peppers
2 cups water
½ cup white vinegar
½ cup brown sugar
1 medium (120g) onion, chopped
1 small fresh red chilli, chopped
1 tablespoon cornflour
2 tablespoons water, extra

Cut peppers in half lengthways, remove seeds. Place peppers, cut side down, on oven tray. Cook under hot grill until skins blister; cool. Remove and discard skins, chop peppers.

Combine water, vinegar and sugar in large saucepan, stir over heat, without boiling, until sugar is dissolved. Stir in peppers, onion and chilli, bring to boil, simmer, uncovered, for 10 minutes. Stir in blended cornflour and extra water, stir until mixture boils and thickens. Pour into hot sterilised jars; seal when cold.

Makes about 2 cups.

SUGAR-FREE ZUCCHINI RELISH

This will keep refrigerated for 4 weeks.

3 medium (500g) zucchini, chopped
1 medium (120g) onion, chopped
2 cups water
½ cup white vinegar
1 medium (150g) red pepper, chopped
1 tablespoon dry mustard
1 tablespoon artificial sweetener powder
1½ tablespoons cornflour
2 tablespoons water, extra

Combine zucchini, onion, water, vinegar, pepper, mustard and sweetener in large saucepan. Bring to boil, simmer, covered, for about 10 minutes or until zucchini is soft. Stir in blended cornflour and extra water, stir over heat until mixture boils and thickens. Pour into hot sterilised jars; seal when cold.

Makes about 5 cups.

LEFT: Clockwise from back: Apricot Relish, Blackberry Relish, Pepper Relish.
ABOVE: Sugar-Free Zucchini Relish.

Left: Dresser in background and wooden box from Appley Hoare Antiques. Above: Table from Polain Interiors

SAUCES

The beauty of home-made sauces is that they can be as thick or as thin as you like. Simply cook the mixture until it's about the consistency you want, let a tablespoon of the mixture cool to room temperature. Test the consistency again and cook further if not thick enough. These sauces should be kept in the refrigerator after they are opened. Be sure to read our hints for success on page 2 to 5 before you start.

CHILLI PLUM SAUCE

14 medium (1kg) plums, chopped
1¼ cups sugar
2 cups white vinegar
2 small fresh red chillies, chopped
1 teaspoon coarse cooking salt
1 teaspoon ground ginger
½ teaspoon cayenne pepper
8 cloves

Combine plums and stones with remaining ingredients in large saucepan, stir over heat, without boiling, until sugar is dissolved. Bring to boil, simmer, uncovered, stirring occasionally, for about 40 minutes or until mixture is pulpy; strain.

Return mixture to pan, bring to boil, simmer, uncovered, for about 10 minutes or until mixture is slightly thickened. Pour into hot sterilised jars; seal when cold.

Makes about 3 cups.

PLUM SAUCE

20 medium (1½kg) plums, pitted, chopped
1½ cups brown sugar, firmly packed
2 cups brown vinegar
1 teaspoon cloves
2 cinnamon sticks
2 star anise
5cm piece fresh ginger, peeled, bruised

Combine plums, sugar and vinegar in large saucepan, stir over heat, without boiling, until sugar is dissolved. Tie cloves, cinnamon, star anise and ginger in piece of muslin; add to pan. Bring to boil, simmer, uncovered, stirring occasionally, for about 45 minutes or until thick. Discard muslin bag. Pour into hot sterilised jars; seal when cold.

Makes about 3 cups.

GREEN TOMATO SAUCE

10 medium (1kg) green tomatoes, chopped
4 green shallots, chopped
½ cup water
1 tablespoon caraway seeds
2 teaspoons turmeric
2 teaspoons mixed spice
½ teaspoon ground ginger
1 cup water, extra
1½ cups sugar
1 cup brown vinegar

Combine tomatoes, shallots and water in large saucepan, bring to boil, simmer, covered, for about 20 minutes or until tomatoes are pulpy. Blend or process mixture in several batches until smooth, return to pan. Stir in remaining ingredients, stir over heat, without boiling, until sugar is dissolved. Bring to boil, simmer, uncovered, stirring occasionally, for about 45 minutes or until mixture is thick. Pour sauce into hot sterilised jars; seal when cold.

Makes about 5 cups.

RIGHT: Clockwise from front: Plum Sauce, Green Tomato Sauce, Chilli Plum Sauce.
Dresser from Appley Hoare Antiques

MUSTARD SAUCE

½ cup oil
¼ cup white mustard seeds, crushed
4 eggs
¼ cup sugar
1½ tablespoons dry mustard
1 teaspoon coarse cooking salt
½ teaspoon cracked black peppercorns
2 teaspoons plain flour
1 cup white vinegar

Heat oil in pan, add seeds, cook until lightly browned; cool.

Blend or process eggs, sugar, dry mustard, salt, peppercorns and flour until smooth. With motor operating, pour in vinegar in a thin stream, then pour in mustard seed mixture in a thin stream.

Transfer mixture to pan, stir over heat until mixture boils and thickens slightly. Pour sauce into hot sterilised jars; seal when cold.

Makes about 2 cups.

BARBECUE SAUCE

2 tablespoons oil
2 cloves garlic, crushed
2 medium (240g) onions, chopped
1 small fresh red chilli, chopped
4 medium (400g) ripe tomatoes, chopped
1 celery stick, chopped
1 large (200g) apple, chopped
½ cup dry red wine
2 tablespoons brown sugar
1 tablespoon seeded mustard
¼ teaspoon coarse cooking salt
¼ teaspoon ground black pepper
1 tablespoon brown vinegar

Heat oil in saucepan, add garlic, onions and chilli, cook until onions are soft. Stir in remaining ingredients, bring to boil, simmer, uncovered, stirring occasionally, for about 30 minutes or until mixture is thick. Blend or process mixture until smooth, push through fine sieve; discard pulp. Pour sauce into hot sterilised jars; seal when cold.

Makes about 2 cups.

TOMATO AND CHILLI SAUCE

3 cloves garlic
1½ tablespoons pimentos
3 teaspoons cloves
2 teaspoons black peppercorns
15 medium (1½kg) ripe tomatoes, peeled, chopped
1½ cups sugar
⅔ cup white vinegar
2 teaspoons coarse cooking salt
3 medium fresh red chillies, chopped

Tie garlic, pimentos, cloves and peppercorns in piece of muslin. Combine remaining ingredients with muslin bag in large saucepan, stir over heat, without boiling until sugar is dissolved.

Bring to boil, simmer, uncovered, stirring occasionally, for about 45 minutes or until mixture thickens slightly. Discard muslin bag. Blend or process mixture in several batches until smooth. Pour sauce into hot sterilised jars; seal when cold.

Makes about 3 cups.

SPICY SAUCE

20 medium (2kg) ripe tomatoes, chopped
¼ teaspoon cayenne pepper
1 medium (120g) onion, chopped
¼ cup sugar
1 cup brown vinegar
2 teaspoons coarse cooking salt
½ teaspoon ground allspice
½ teaspoon ground cinnamon
½ teaspoon ground cloves
½ teaspoon ground ginger

Combine tomatoes, pepper, onion and sugar in large saucepan. Bring to boil, simmer, uncovered, stirring occasionally, for about 30 minutes or until thick. Blend or process mixture in batches until smooth. Strain sauce into pan, stir in vinegar, salt and spices. Bring to boil, simmer, uncovered, for 5 minutes. Pour into hot sterilised jars; seal when cold.

Makes about 4 cups (1litre).

LEFT: Clockwise from back: Mustard Sauce, Barbecue Sauce, Tomato and Chilli Sauce, Spicy Sauce.

Small glass jugs and wooden board from Shop 3, Balmain; tiles from Country Floors

MILD TOMATO SAUCE

30 medium (3kg) ripe tomatoes, chopped
3 medium (360g) onions, chopped
2 large (400g) apples, chopped
1 cup white vinegar
1 cup water
1 nutmeg
2 cups sugar

Combine tomatoes, onions, apples, vinegar, water and nutmeg in large saucepan. Bring to boil, simmer, uncovered, stirring occasionally, for about 1 hour or until thick. Add sugar, stir over heat, without boiling, until sugar is dissolved. Blend or process mixture in several batches until smooth; push through fine sieve. Discard pulp. Pour into hot sterilised jars; seal when cold.

Makes about 6 cups (1½ litres).

RICH FRUIT SAUCE

17 medium (1¾kg) tomatoes, chopped
5 large (1kg) apples, chopped
4 medium (480g) onions, chopped
1½ cups (250g) dates, chopped
5 cups (750g) raisins
1 litre (4 cups) white vinegar
1 teaspoon mixed spice
2 teaspoons white mustard seeds
¼ teaspoon cayenne pepper
2 small fresh red chillies, chopped
2 cups brown sugar, firmly packed

Combine all ingredients except sugar in large saucepan. Bring to boil, simmer, covered, for about 1 hour or until mixture is pulpy.

Push mixture through coarse sieve, return mixture to pan, stir in sugar. Stir over heat, without boiling, until sugar is dissolved. Bring to boil, simmer, uncovered, stirring occasionally, for about 1 hour or until sauce thickens slightly. Pour into hot sterilised jars; seal when cold.

Makes about 8 cups (2 litres).

HOME-MADE WORCESTERSHIRE SAUCE

3 cups brown vinegar
½ cup treacle
½ cup plum jam
1 small (75g) onion, chopped
1 clove garlic, crushed
¼ teaspoon chilli powder
1 teaspoon ground allspice
¼ teaspoon ground cloves
¼ teaspoon cayenne pepper

Combine all ingredients in large saucepan. Stir over heat until mixture boils, simmer, uncovered, for 1 hour, stirring occasionally. Strain mixture into hot sterilised jars; seal when cold.

Makes about 2 cups.

ABOVE: From back: Rich Fruit Sauce, Mild Tomato Sauce.
RIGHT: Home-Made Worcestershire Sauce.

Above: Wooden container from Appley Hoare.
Right: Glass bottles from The Australian East India Co.; tiles from Northbridge Ceramic & Marble Centre

DAD'S FAVOURITE SAUCE

10 medium (1kg) ripe tomatoes, peeled, chopped
4 large (800g) apples, peeled, chopped
4 medium (480g) onions, chopped
2 cups sugar
1/4 cup Worcestershire sauce
2 tablespoons golden syrup
2 cups cider vinegar
2 cups water
2 teaspoons coarse cooking salt
2 teaspoons mixed spice
2 teaspoons dry mustard
1 teaspoon ground black pepper
1 tablespoon curry powder
2 tablespoons cornflour
1/4 cup water, extra

Combine all ingredients except cornflour and extra water in large saucepan. Stir over heat, without boiling, until sugar is dissolved. Bring to boil, simmer, uncovered, stirring occasionally, for about 1 hour or until sauce is thick. Blend or process mixture in batches until smooth. Return to pan, stir in blended cornflour and extra water, stir until mixture boils and thickens. Pour into hot sterilised jars; seal when cold.

Makes about 6 cups (1 1/2 litres).

RASPBERRY CIDER SAUCE

2kg raspberries
2 1/2 cups cider vinegar
1 teaspoon French mustard
1/2 teaspoon mixed spice
1 2/3 cups sugar

Combine raspberries and vinegar in large saucepan. Bring to boil, simmer, uncovered, for 15 minutes. Stir in mustard and spice, simmer further 30 minutes. Strain mixture into clean pan through fine sieve; discard seeds.

Stir in sugar, stir over heat, without boiling, until sugar is dissolved. Bring to boil, simmer, uncovered, stirring occasionally, for 30 minutes. Pour into hot sterilised jars; seal when cold.

Makes about 4 cups (1 litre).

RIGHT: From left: Dad's Favourite Sauce, Raspberry Cider Sauce.

BUTTERS & SPREADS

We like to use unsalted butter where required in these recipes, but regular salted butter works just as well.
Most of the butters in this section need to be cooked gently over simmering water. Use either a double saucepan or a large heatproof bowl (glass or china are best) placed over a saucepan of simmering water. The simmering water should not touch the base of the bowl or the base of the top half of the double saucepan. The mixtures must not boil, but will thicken like a custard. The butter will set the butters firmer when cold. All recipes will keep for several weeks in the refrigerator.

CHERRY LEMON SPREAD

1¼kg cherries, pitted
½ cup water
2 cups sugar, approximately
½ teaspoon grated lemon rind
2 tablespoons lemon juice

Combine cherries and water in large saucepan, bring to boil, simmer, covered, for about 15 minutes or until cherries are soft. Push cherries through sieve, discard skins. Measure cherry mixture, allow 1 cup sugar to each cup of cherry mixture. Return cherry mixture and sugar to pan, add rind and juice. Stir over heat, without boiling, until sugar is dissolved.

Bring to boil, boil, uncovered, for about 15 minutes or until mixture will spread when cold. Pour into hot sterilised jars; seal when cold.

Makes about 2 cups.

PASSIONFRUIT LEMON BUTTER

You will need about 12 passionfruit.
4 eggs, beaten, strained
¾ cup castor sugar
2 teaspoons grated lemon rind
½ cup lemon juice
125g butter, chopped
1 cup passionfruit pulp

Combine all ingredients in top half of double saucepan or in heatproof bowl. Stir over simmering water until mixture thickly coats the back of a wooden spoon. Pour into hot sterilised jars; seal when cold.

Makes about 3 cups.

CITRUS SPREAD

2 large (440g) oranges
1 medium (180g) lemon
1 medium (85g) lime
1 litre (4 cups) water
7 cups (1¾kg) sugar

Blend or process unpeeled, chopped fruit, including seeds, with the water in batches until finely chopped.

Transfer mixture to large saucepan, add sugar, stir over heat, without boiling, until sugar is dissolved. Bring to boil, boil, uncovered, without stirring, for about 15 minutes or until mixture will spread when cold. Pour into hot sterilised jars; seal when cold.

Makes about 8 cups.

RIGHT: Clockwise from front: Cherry Lemon Spread, Passionfruit Lemon Butter, Citrus Spread.
Table and wooden trays from The Country Trader

DARK PLUM SPREAD

28 medium (2kg) plums, halved
1 cup water
6 cups (1½kg) sugar, approximately
¼ cup lemon juice

Combine plums with stones and water in large saucepan, bring to boil, simmer, covered, for about 30 minutes or until plums are pulpy. Push mixture through a sieve; reserve liquid, discard pulp.

Measure liquid, allow 1 cup sugar to each cup of liquid. Combine liquid, sugar and juice in pan. Bring to boil, boil, uncovered, for about 10 minutes or until mixture will spread when cold. Pour into hot sterilised jars; seal when cold.

Makes about 8 cups.

BANANA SPREAD

3 medium (500g) ripe bananas
⅓ cup lemon juice
125g butter, chopped
4 egg yolks

Blend or process bananas until smooth. Combine bananas, juice, butter and egg yolks in top half of double saucepan or in heatproof bowl. Stir over simmering water until mixture thickly coats the back of a wooden spoon. Pour into hot sterilised jars; seal when cold.

Makes about 2 cups.

LEMON GINGER BUTTER

6 egg yolks
¾ cup castor sugar
1 teaspoon grated lemon rind
1 cup lemon juice
1½ teaspoons ground ginger
¼ cup glace ginger, finely chopped
180g butter, chopped

Combine egg yolks and sugar in top half of double saucepan or in heatproof bowl, stir in rind, juice, gingers and butter. Stir over simmering water until mixture thickly coats the back of a wooden spoon. Pour into hot sterilised jars; seal when cold.

Makes about 2 cups.

LEMON AND LIME BUTTER

180g butter, chopped
2 cups castor sugar
½ cup lemon juice
1 teaspoon grated lime rind
⅓ cup lime juice
4 eggs, beaten, strained

Combine all ingredients in top half of double saucepan or in heatproof bowl. Stir over simmering water until mixture thickly coats the back of a wooden spoon. Pour into hot sterilised jars; seal when cold.

Makes about 3 cups.

ORANGE PASSIONFRUIT BUTTER

5 eggs, beaten, strained
¾ cup castor sugar
2 passionfruit
3 teaspoons grated orange rind
½ cup orange juice
¼ cup water
125g butter, chopped

Combine eggs and sugar in top half of double saucepan or in heatproof bowl. Stir in passionfruit pulp and remaining ingredients. Stir mixture over simmering water until mixture thickly coats the back of a wooden spoon. Pour into hot sterilised jars; seal when cold.

Makes about 3 cups.

LEFT: From left: Dark Plum Spread, Banana Spread.
ABOVE: From top: Lemon and Lime Butter, Lemon Ginger Butter, Orange Passionfruit Butter.

Above: Cupboard from Flossoms; plate from Burgundy Antiques

NUTTY PLUM SPREAD

14 medium (1kg) plums
2 cups brown sugar, firmly packed
1/4 cup orange juice
1/4 cup lemon juice
1/2 cup pecans or walnuts, chopped
1/2 cup glace ginger, chopped

Halve plums, discard stones, chop plums roughly. Combine plums, sugar and juices in large saucepan. Stir over heat, without boiling, until sugar is dissolved, bring to boil, simmer, uncovered, stirring occasionally, for about 20 minutes or until mixture is thick and will spread when cold. Stir in nuts and ginger. Pour into hot sterilised jars; seal when cold.

Makes about 3 cups.

PLUM BUTTER

7 medium (500g) plums, pitted, chopped
1/4 cup lemon juice
4 eggs, beaten, strained
3/4 cup castor sugar
125g butter, chopped

Combine plums and juice in large saucepan. Bring to boil, simmer, covered, for about 20 minutes or until plums are soft. Push plum mixture through sieve. Discard pulp.

Combine eggs and sugar in top half of double saucepan or in heatproof bowl; stir in plum mixture and butter. Stir over simmering water until mixture thickly coats the back of a wooden spoon. Pour mixture into hot sterilised jars; seal when cold.

Makes about 3 cups.

RASPBERRY RED SPREAD

250g raspberries
2 cups castor sugar
1/3 cup cornflour
2 eggs, beaten, strained
2 tablespoons grated lemon rind
2/3 cup lemon juice
80g butter, chopped

Blend or process berries until smooth. Combine berries and remaining ingredients in saucepan, stir over heat until mixture boils and thickens. Pour mixture into hot sterilised jars; seal when cold.

Makes about 3 cups.

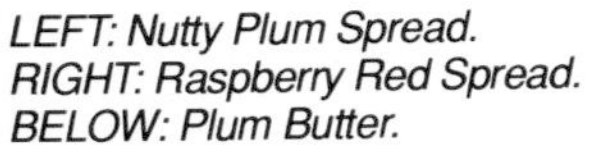

LEFT: Nutty Plum Spread.
RIGHT: Raspberry Red Spread.
BELOW: Plum Butter.

Left: Setting from The Prop House; background from Prompt Scenery Services. Right: Candles from Home & Garden. Below: Wooden plate from Corso de Fiori; china plate from Shop 3, Balmain

You can make superb liqueurs by adding fruit to a sweetened spirit base. They must be stored in a cool dark place at all stages of preparation, and must be sealed tightly to prevent evaporation. At some stage in the making, as specified in the recipes, fruit is macerated in the spirit to develop luscious flavour; very little cooking is involved.

Most liqueurs should be kept for at least 6 weeks after bottling. Exceptions are those mixed with fruit and left to stand for a period before bottling, for example, cherry brandy liqueur.

For a liqueur made with berries, you can use fresh or frozen varieties with equally good results.

Don't waste the fruit from the liqueur; serve it with cream or ice-cream for a special treat.

PEACH CITRUS LIQUEUR

3 medium (500g) peaches, halved, pitted
¾ cup sugar
6cm piece orange rind
1 cup brandy
¼ cup Cointreau
1 cinnamon stick

Chop peaches roughly; combine in large bowl with sugar, rind, brandy, liqueur and cinnamon, cover tightly; refrigerate mixture for 1 week.

Strain mixture through fine cloth, pour into sterilised bottle; seal.

Makes about 2 cups.

APRICOT WINE LIQUEUR

12 medium (500g) apricots, halved, pitted
2 cups sugar
1 litre (4 cups) dry white wine
2 cups gin

Combine apricots, sugar and wine in large saucepan. Stir over heat, without boiling, until sugar is dissolved, bring to boil, simmer, covered, 5 minutes; cool. Transfer mixture to large bowl, stir in gin, cover tightly, stand liqueur in a cool dark place for 5 days.

Strain mixture through fine cloth, reserve liquid; discard pulp. Pour into sterilised bottles; seal.

Makes about 7 cups (1¾ litres).

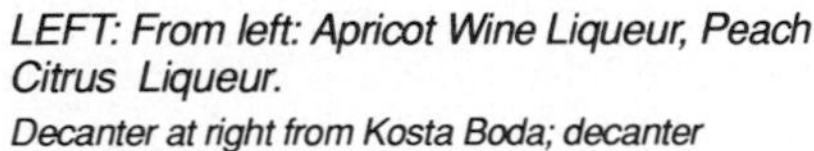

LEFT: From left: Apricot Wine Liqueur, Peach Citrus Liqueur.

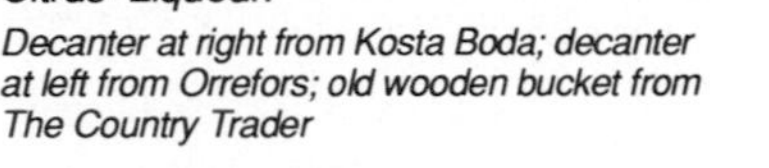

Decanter at right from Kosta Boda; decanter at left from Orrefors; old wooden bucket from The Country Trader

BRANDIED ORANGE LIQUEUR

3 large (660g) oranges
1 cup brandy
1¼ cups sugar
¼ teaspoon ground coriander
¼ teaspoon ground cinnamon

Peel rind thinly from oranges, using vegetable peeler; finely chop rind. Squeeze juice from oranges; you will need 1 cup juice. Combine rind, juice, brandy, sugar, coriander and cinnamon in bowl, cover tightly, stand 2 days; stirring occasionally.

Strain mixture through fine cloth, reserve liquid; discard pulp. Pour liquid into sterilised bottle; seal.

Makes about 2 cups.

PEAR LIQUEUR

3 cups sugar
1 cup water
7 medium (1kg) pears
2 cups vodka

Combine sugar and water in large saucepan, stir over heat, without boiling, until sugar is dissolved. Peel, core and slice pears, add to pan, bring to boil, simmer, covered, for about 15 minutes or until pears are transparent; cool in sugar syrup to room temperature.

Strain pear mixture through fine cloth, reserve liquid; discard pulp. Combine pear liquid with vodka in jug, pour into sterilised bottles; seal.

Makes about 5 cups (1¼ litres).

CHERRY BRANDY LIQUEUR

500g cherries, pitted
1 cup sugar
3 cups brandy
1 cinnamon stick

Combine cherries and sugar in large sterilised jar, cover with tight-fitting lid, stand 2 to 3 days; shake jar daily until juice begins to appear.

Add brandy and cinnamon to jar, seal tightly, stand 3 months in cool dark place, shaking jar occasionally.

Strain cherries through fine cloth, reserve liquid, discard pulp. Pour liquid into sterilised bottles; seal.

Makes about 4 cups (1 litre).

ABOVE: From left: Brandied Orange Liqueur, Pear Liqueur.
RIGHT: Cherry Brandy Liqueur.

Above: China from Mikasa; table and tray from Burgundy Antiques; decanter and glasses from Waterford. Right: Decanter and glasses from Orrefors.

STRAWBERRY LIQUEUR

500g strawberries
2 cups gin
1 tablespoon grenadine syrup
¾ cup castor sugar

Hull strawberries, chop roughly. Combine strawberries, gin and grenadine in large bowl, cover, refrigerate 2 days.

Add sugar to bowl, stand, uncovered, for about 2 hours or until sugar is dissolved, stirring occasionally. Strain mixture through fine cloth into large jug, reserve liquid; discard pulp. Pour into sterilised bottle; seal.

Makes about 3 cups.

BLACKBERRY LIQUEUR

1kg blackberries
4 cups (1kg) sugar
2 cups water
1 teaspoon ground nutmeg
3 cups brandy
1 cup vodka

Combine berries, sugar, water and nutmeg in large saucepan. Stir over heat, without boiling, until sugar is dissolved. Bring to boil, simmer, uncovered, for about 30 minutes or until reduced by about three-quarters. Strain liquid through fine cloth, reserve liquid; discard pulp. Combine liquid, brandy and vodka in jug, pour into sterilised bottles; seal.

Makes about 4 cups (1 litre).

ORANGE CALVADOS LIQUEUR

3 large (660g) oranges
1 cinnamon stick
700ml bottle Calvados
1½ cups castor sugar

Peel rind thinly from oranges, using vegetable peeler; cut rind into thin strips. Combine rind, cinnamon and Calvados in bowl, cover; refrigerate for 1 week.

Strain orange mixture through fine cloth into bowl, discard rind and cinnamon. Add sugar, stir until dissolved. Pour into sterilised bottle; seal.

Makes about 3 cups.

ABOVE: Clockwise from back: Orange Calvados Liqueur, Strawberry Liqueur, Blackberry Liqueur.

GLOSSARY

Some terms, names and alternatives are included here to help everyone understand and use our recipes perfectly.

ALCOHOL: is optional but gives a particular flavour. Omit alcohol, if preferred.

ALLSPICE: pimento in ground form.

AMARETTO: is an almond-flavoured liqueur.

CALVADOS: an apple-flavoured brandy.

CHILLIES: fresh chillies are available in many types and sizes. The small ones (bird's eye or bird peppers) are the hottest. Use tight-fitting gloves when handling and chopping fresh chillies as they can burn your skin. The seeds are the hottest part, so remove them if you want to reduce the heat content of recipes.

CHILLI POWDER: the Asian variety is the hottest and is made from ground red chillies; it can be used as a substitute for fresh chillies in the proportion of ½ teaspoon ground chilli powder to 1 medium chilli.

CITRIC ACID: is commonly found in most fruits, especially limes and lemons. Commercial citric acid helps to accentuate the acid flavour of fruit; it does not act as a preservative.

COINTREAU: is an orange-flavoured liqueur.

FEIJOA: a small round fruit with green or brownish-yellow skin and pale pink flesh (similar to guava).

FRAMBOISE: is a raspberry-flavoured liqueur. Creme de Framboises is sweeter.

GARAM MASALA: there are many variations of the combinations of cardamom, cinnamon, cloves, coriander, cumin and nutmeg used to make up this spice used often in Indian cooking. Sometimes pepper is used to make a hot variation. Garam masala is readily available in jars.

GELFIX: is an imported pectin preparation used for the setting of jams and jellies; it is available in packets of 3 x 20g pouches (20g is the equivalent of 1½ tablespoons).

GINGER: fresh green or root ginger; scrape away skin and it is ready to chop, grate or slice as required. A piece of peeled ginger can be used unchopped for flavouring, as required.

GRAND MARNIER: an orange-flavoured liqueur.

GRENADINE SYRUP: non-alcoholic flavouring made from pomegranate juice; bright red in colour. Imitation cordial is also available.

JAMSETTA: is an Australian-made jam-setting mixture with pectin; it is available in 50g packets.

KIRSCH: a cherry-flavoured liqueur.

MUSTARD SEEDS: tiny seeds used in curries, pickling and making mustard; seeds can be black (spicy and piquant), brown (less piquant) or white (yellow in colour and milder in flavour).

ONIONS, PICKLING: very small, brown-skinned variety.

ORANGES, SEVILLE: very tart in flavour; suitable only for jam-making.

PECTIN: is a carbohydrate present in certain fruits and vegetables which, when combined with sugar, helps a jam, jelly or marmalade to set or jell. Commercial pectin helps when there is not enough natural pectin. Also see pages 2 to 5 for more information.

PIMENTO: allspice.

RUM: we used dark (underproof) rum.

SALT, COARSE COOKING: contains no anti-caking agent and is used as a seasoning and as a preservative.

SAUTERNES: a sweet white wine originating in the Sauternes area of France.

SWEETENER: can be in liquid or powdered form and contains no sugar.

TAMARILLO: dark red egg-shaped fruit from a tree native to Peru. The skin is astringent and should be peeled. Drop tamarillo into hot water, let stand 3 to 4 minutes then peel skin with a sharp knife.

TARTARIC ACID: is used in making sweets and preserves to prevent the crystallisation of the sugar.

WHISKY: we used a good quality Scotch whisky.

WINE, SWEET WHITE: we used a moselle.

Cup and Spoon Measurements

Recipes in this book use this standard metric equipment approved by Standards Australia:

(a) 250 millilitre cup for measuring liquids. A litre jug (capacity 4 cups) is also available.

(b) a graduated set of four cups – measuring 1 cup, half, third and quarter cup – for items such as flour, sugar, etc. When measuring in these fractional cups level off at the brim.

(c) a graduated set of four spoons: tablespoon (20 millilitre liquid capacity), teaspoon (5 millilitre), half and quarter teaspoons. The Australian, British and American teaspoon each has 5ml capacity.

Approximate Cup and Spoon Conversion Chart

Australian	American & British
1 cup	1¼ cups
¾ cup	1 cup
⅔ cup	¾ cup
½ cup	⅔ cup
⅓ cup	½ cup
¼ cup	⅓ cup
2 tablespoons	¼ cup
1 tablespoon	3 teaspoons

Oven Temperatures

ELECTRIC	C°	F°
Very slow	120	250
Slow	150	300
Moderately slow	160-180	325-350
Moderate	180-200	375-400
Moderately hot	210-230	425-450
Hot	240-250	475-500
Very hot	260	525-550

GAS	C°	F°
Very slow	120	250
Slow	150	300
Moderately slow	160	325
Moderate	180	350
Moderately hot	190	375
Hot	200	400
Very hot	230	450

ALL SPOON MEASUREMENTS ARE LEVEL. WE HAVE USED LARGE EGGS WITH AN AVERAGE WEIGHT OF 61g EACH IN ALL RECIPES.

INDEX

A

B

C

D

E,F

G

H,I

J

L

M,N

O

P

Q,R

S

T

V,W,Z

GRAPHIC STYLE